Brown Bag Lessons

The Magic of Bullet Writing

By

Eric R. Jaren
Chief Master Sergeant, USAF, Retired

Edited by

Don Alexander
Master Chief, USN, Retired

Air University Press
Maxwell Air Force Base, Alabama

Project Editor
Belinda Bazinet

Copy Editor
Tammi Dacus

Cover Art, Book Design, and Illustrations
L. Susan Fair

Composition and Prepress Production
Vivian D. O'Neal

Print Preparation and Distribution
Diane Clark

AIR UNIVERSITY PRESS

Director and Publisher
Dr. Ernest Allan Rockwell

Air University Press
600 Chennault Circle, Building 1405
Maxwell AFB, AL 36112-6010

https://www.airuniversity.af.edu/AUPress/

Facebook:
https://www.facebook.com/AirUnivPress
and
Twitter: https://twitter.com/aupress

Library of Congress Cataloging-in-Publication Data

Names: Jaren, Eric R., 1964- author. | Air University (U.S.). Press, publisher.
Title: Brown bag lessons : the magic of bullet writing / Eric R. Jaren.
Other titles: Magic of Bullet Writing
Description: First edition. | Maxwell Air Force Base, Alabama : Air University Press, [2018]
Identifiers: LCCN 2017052719| ISBN 9781585662784 | ISBN 158566278X
Subjects: LCSH: United States—Armed Forces—Promotions—Evaluation. | United States—Armed Forces—Promotions. | Employees—Rating of—United States. | Performance awards—United States.
Classification: LCC UB323 .J37 2018 | DDC 808.06/6355—dc23 | SUDOC D 301.26/6:B 87
LC record available at https://lccn.loc.gov/2017052719

First Printing December 2017
Second Printing April 2018
Third Printing August 2020
Copyright © 2012 by Eric R. Jaren

Disclaimer

Opinions, conclusions, and recommendations expressed or implied within are solely those of the authors and do not necessarily represent the official policy or position of the organizations with which they are associated or the views of the Air University Press, Air University, United States Air Force, Department of Defense, or any other US government agency. This publication is cleared for public release and unlimited distribution.

Contents

List of Illustrations	*v*
Foreword	*vii*
About the Author	*ix*
Acknowledgments	*xi*
Preface	*xiii*
Introduction	*xv*

Part 1 Timeless Lessons

1	Genesis	3
2	A Better Mousetrap	7
3	A Consistent Approach	11

Part 2 The *Magic*

4	Bullet Formats	17
5	Performance Levels	29
6	The Performance Scale	39

Part 3 Practice Makes Perfect

7	Scoring Mechanics	53
8	Top 10 Writing Traps	59
9	Perfect Practice Makes Perfect	67

Part 4 Conducting Boards

10	You Just Can't Make This Up	105
	Abbreviations	109
	Appendix	111

List of Illustrations

Figure

1	Tactical-Operational-Strategic	21
2	Tactical-Tactical-Tactical	21
3	Tactical-Tactical-Operational	22
4	Tactical-Tactical-Strategic	22
5	Performance-level model	31

Table

1	Performance-level scores	54

Foreword

What leader in any organization hasn't sat back and internally screamed, "There has to be a better way!" Reader beware, there is a better way. What I inherently knew as a member of US Navy E-7 through E-9 selection boards, CMSgt Eric R. Jaren has captured in a systematic process useful for every level of leadership. The consistency in the approach embodies reflective, thoughtful consideration to capture the truth and proper context of every person's accomplishments. The use of performance levels is not confined to any specific military service. Indeed, it's universal in application in any business and culture. The addition of this model into company grade officer (CGO) and senior noncommissioned officer (SNCO) combined curriculum underpins the operational and long-term strategic importance for the force.

This model was implemented into the Senior Noncommissioned Officer Academy (SNCOA) and CGO curriculum as a "best practice" for meeting the responsibility to mentor institutional competencies directly impacting the careers of the team. Feedback from students, scholar-warriors, substantiates the model. The model provides unadulterated feedback in mentoring and maintains integrity with promotion and award processes. From this, leadership, followership, and the core doctrine of developing Airmen are assured. No other presentation media in 33 days of curriculum was asked for by more students to take back for use in operational units.

DON ALEXANDER
Command Master Chief, USN, retired
Director of Curriculum
Air Force SNCOA

About the Author

After 30 years of leading our nation's Airmen, Chief Master Sergeant Eric R. Jaren's powerful fervor to write *Brown Bag Lessons, The Magic of Bullet Writing* is a reflection of his passion for developing, coaching, and mentoring all Airmen. Chief Jaren literally influenced the lives of thousands through his seminars and motivational talks about taking care of Airmen and their families and how to communicate their accomplishments through the written word. With the Chief, it always comes back around to the core focus of developing leaders. The *magic* of this masterpiece is that these timeless brown bag lessons can be used by any organization—both military and civilian. Chief Jaren's personal mantra has always been "Find a Need, Meet a Need," and his desire for you is that the struggle to write comes to an end. Are you ready for the *magic*?

Chief Jaren retired from the US Air Force in 2012. Formerly the Command Chief Master Sergeant for Air Force Materiel Command's 13,000+ enlisted Airmen and their families, Chief Jaren's 30-year career brought him from the flight line as an aircraft mechanic to the front line as a senior Air Force leader. He's a warrior Airman who's deployed worldwide, including support of Operations Desert Storm and Desert Shield, Iraqi Freedom, and Enduring Freedom. Chief Jaren holds a master's degree in business administration from Trident University and an executive certificate in negotiation from the University of Notre Dame.

Acknowledgments

By associating with wise people you will become wise yourself.
—Menander, Greek dramatist

In the year preceding my retirement, friends, peers, and colleagues asked that I capture these techniques so they wouldn't be lost with my departure. So, I put pen to paper in the hope that future generations won't have to relearn what is already successful. Between the covers you'll find contributions from people cut from the same cloth. Please allow me to give credit where credit is due.

Thanks also to Thomas Jones and Manuel Sarmiento who offered critical input used to explain the origins of the concept presented; to Alexander Perry, Anderson Aupiu, and Christopher Powell—my peers, mentors, confidants, and dear friends—who were proponents offering feedback to the original principles; and to my dear friends Andrew Hollis, Casey Schoettmer, and Sean Chaplin. I owe much gratitude for their efforts as contributing editors and thoughtful suggestions to the substance.

A very special thank you to my "ambassador of *quan*," Mark Brejcha, for writing the "About the Author" section.[1] I'd also like to acknowledge Robert Stroebel, Dave Gilmore, James Martin, Wesley Riopel, Alan Braden, Edward Ames, James Shepherd, Michele Owczarski, and Justin Deisch for thoughtful contributions and being incredible advocates, proponents, and mentors who invest in their people; and to Mark Bennett and Don Alexander for taking the principles to the Squadron Officer School (SOS) and SNCOA.

A special thanks to Don for his efforts as a contributing editor, writing the foreword and accepting the responsibility to prepare this manuscript for submission to Air University Press. I cannot thank you enough for your selfless efforts.

Warmest regards for all my mentors and teammates.

Note

1. Reference phrase used in the 1996 movie Jerry Maguire with Tom Cruise and Cuba Gooding Jr. "Jerry, you are the ambassador of *quan*." The meaning of quan, in this instance, meaning to be at one with a particular thing or skill.

Preface

Start with why.
—Simon Sinek, motivational speaker/author

Brown Bag Lessons, The Magic of Bullet Writing is the first book in a series on leadership. This book centers on effective bullet writing and guarantees immediate improvement. Skillful writing doesn't have to be difficult.

No other book approaches writing the way this book does, and no other book teaches these techniques. After reading this book, you will fully understand how to write bullets and "why" every word matters.

In 2003 the author created a seminar to teach a fair and consistent process to evaluate recognition packages. This seminar transformed an entire organization within six months. Since then, the techniques have decisively transformed the writing, recognition, and promotions of every organization applying them.

The practices in this book continue to positively impact the Air Force and sister services through professional military education. In addition, the concepts have helped transitioning service members and college students better communicate acquired capabilities and competencies on their résumés. Read on to discover the "magic" and open your eyes to a brand new way to look at writing.

Recent changes to the US Air Force enlisted promotion system make it more important to document your very best accomplishments. Under the new system, points come from the most recent enlisted performance reports (EPR). The new system requires fewer lines, so Airmen must communicate the best accomplishments and not just words that fill the white space. This *Magic of Bullet Writing* will ensure you know how to articulate not just what you are doing but also convey your strongest competencies and capabilities so the promotion board can fully assess your potential. Training materials that correspond to the lessons in this book are available for free download at http://www.brownbaglessons.com.

Are you ready for the *magic*?

Introduction

The task of leadership is not to put greatness into people, but to elicit it, for the greatness is there already.

—John Buchan, Scottish novelist, historian, and politician

Developing, coaching, and mentoring are my passion—investing in others has brought more satisfaction than any individual accomplishment. So, it would seem the time and energy spent helping others to succeed is returned twofold in contentment. That is what likely inspired my mentors to make an impact early in my career.

While I don't consider myself a "writer," I do consider myself a coach and mentor—someone who is willing to help others build a brighter career. I have been presenting professional development seminars for many years, as a job requirement but also, more importantly, as a personal passion.

From 2002 to present I shared techniques of military writing in every forum imaginable. Whether presenting in a base theater, a conference center, or via my laptop in a hotel room in Okinawa, Japan, developing people is what makes me go.

The genesis of this book's material was initially shared with small groups. Through the years, audiences grew from dozens to more than 500 people at a time. During the last few years, the seminars reached tens of thousands.. Like a light switched on, time and again, people attending the seminar said, "I get it."

This system has the potential not only to revolutionize how we approach bullets but also to transform our entire merit-based system. In January 2012 the Air Force recognized the force-wide value and inculcated the concepts into the SNCOA and SOS curricula. Before being discontinued in 2014, over 28,300 students received this information through the course curriculum.

> I wholeheartedly recommend the principles outlined in this book. Our education institutions incorporated these principles into curriculum for more than 5,000 company grade and senior non-commissioned officers annually.
>
> There are three main reasons why each leader should embrace these techniques. First, the writer is forced to ensure each bullet meets a set standard. Second, it creates consistency and structure within the Air Force. By applying these sound principles, leaders will assist with the evolution of our performance evaluation system, awards boards, and even promotion boards by creating a systematic approach to bullet writing to remove ambiguity within each

INTRODUCTION

process. And third, these techniques add credibility to our system. Each bullet will now have merit. Therefore, every board member can easily assign a point value to each bullet and be able to support the overall rating to fellow board members. No longer will there be an ambiguous guess at how a board member arrived at their rating. Each time I use these techniques on boards, it helps identify the most deserving person.

—CMSgt Mark Bennett, USAF, retired

The most distinctive part is that these techniques do not teach through conventional methods. These principles teach from the opposite point of view, from the evaluation side for clear understanding.

I have observed thousands struggling to compose, articulate, and formulate statements for recognition packages and performance appraisals. People spent countless hours in frustration because they were writing in vain, knowing that someone higher up would drench the draft in red ink and send it back to rework with the document looking nothing like the original. This frustration is still prevalent today.

I simply cannot say it more clearly—"The struggle to write comes to an end!" The countless hours of rewriting bullets stops here.

> When I was at base level, I supervised military and civilian staff members. I struggled to write the type of performance and award bullets this book teaches. If I had received instruction of this caliber earlier in my career, my packages would have been stronger and my staff properly recognized. The techniques taught in this book should be included in the curriculum for all supervisory training programs.
>
> —Shelly Owczarski, DAF, retired
> Chief, Air Force Materiel Command
> Voluntary Education Program

Those who learn this method, whether they have been a supervisor for two or 22 years, express how beneficial it would have been if the techniques were accessible much earlier in their career. Some were adamantly upset because they struggled for so long.

> Since learning this process I've authored two major command, eight numbered Air Force, and over 100 wing and group level to this process. I still use the training slides given to me by Eric to mentor the men and women in my squadron. All I've received is positive feedback on how the process has helped make them better writers. I'm thankful I'm able to share this standard with the folks in my wing.
>
> —CMSgt Edward Ames, USAF, retired

INTRODUCTION

All supervisors incur a responsibility for counseling, conducting feedback, and documenting performance. The techniques taught in this book directly apply to all of these applications.

The Magic of Bullet Writing saves time by reducing edit and review work by half or more. Productivity increases because backlogged reports are transferred off your desk. Nevertheless, there is more! It also makes your employees more productive because they'll compose reports correctly the first time. The vicious cycle of reports going back and forth ends.

As you begin, I would like to point out a unique aspect of the book. *Brown Bag Notes* are in each chapter. These provide a useful setup to facilitate mentoring sessions.

I am grateful for contributing to a system that has enlightened so many and provided such a return on investment. Please enjoy the book in its entirety.

Part 1

Timeless Lessons

In the movie *The Matrix*, Morpheus asked Neo to choose the blue pill, which offers security and blissful ignorance, or the red pill, which provides freedom and, perhaps painful, truth. Most of us would select the blue pill when it comes to writing. Trust me; the wool has been pulled over our eyes through repetitive bad habit. Reading the first three chapters of this book is like taking the red pill. Your eyes will be opened to the world of writing in a whole new way. Once you know the truth you will see everything differently afterward, just as in the movie.

However, just seeing the truth is not enough. After seeing the Matrix for what it was, Neo had to relearn everything about life. So, the trick is to not just see anew but also to learn anew.

This book includes numerous writing tips, but the premise of the book is to teach a technique called the "*magic*." The best part—you will apply the *magic* in the remaining chapters. It's time to enter the rabbit hole.

Chapter 1

Genesis

Let there be light.

—Genesis 1:3

- *While a promotion may catapult someone to supervisory status, it does not guarantee proficiency in the written word.*
- *An organization can be transformed by teaching how to score recognition packages.*
- *A simple three-step process identifies the strengths and weaknesses of each bullet.*
- *Scoring packages makes you a better writer.*

Effective writing is a major part of supervisory responsibilities, yet very little time is spent actually *learning* how to write effectively. While a promotion may catapult someone to supervisor status, it does not guarantee proficiency in the written word. In 2002, to combat poor writing, I taught a course entitled "How to Write Performance Reports." Regardless of how often the course was taught, there was minimal to no improvement. For 12 months the pile of blue folders holding performance reports on my desk never shrunk.

Unfortunately, many are promoted without the writing proficiency needed for success.

Most supervisors only write one or two performance reports each year. No matter how well intentioned, the majority of supervisors do not have the experience nor the skills to write well, and the writing course wasn't helping. The ability to write is the sum of your entire education, experience, and practice—as well as natural gifts and talents. You cannot teach someone to become a significantly better writer during a one-hour seminar.

Everything changed in 2003. Out of the blue, the group superintendent, 615th Air Mobility Operations Group, CMSgt Manuel Sarmiento, directed a change to the way recognition packages were scored. The new process included noncommissioned officers (NCO) and senior NCOs (SNCO), a practice commonly used across the Air

Force today. Chief "Sam" put out a call for sharp NCOs to participate in the upcoming board. Soon after, replies flooded my inbox and the first volunteer was knocking on my door. He said, "Sergeant Jaren, I volunteer, but I don't know how to score awards. Is there training available?"

I vividly recalled lessons learned during my assignment at the 15th Air Force and knew they needed to be shared. That evening I stayed late to write down practices learned years earlier. In the coming days, several senior leaders—the squadron first sergeant, MSgt Alexander Perry; the operations superintendent, MSgt Christopher Powell; and the operations flight chief, MSgt Anderson Aupiu—contributed effective feedback for the training seminar.

A simple three-step process identifies the strengths and weaknesses of each bullet.

The heart of the training centered on evaluating each accomplishment against the levels of expected performance. The process applied a simple three-step process to evaluate the strength and weakness of each bullet. These levels are explained in later chapters and form the genesis of better writing.

A stunning breakthrough asserted itself soon after delivering the seminars—the blue folders began to go away. The *magic* began. By "scoring" bullets against "levels" of performance, better understanding and writing ensued.

> I first ran into one of Chief Jaren's Brown Bag Lessons by happenstance. I put it on my calendar and convinced myself I was too busy. I planned on skipping it until my boss pointed at the clock and informed me I had somewhere to be. There are moments in your life where you reluctantly hear something that ends up changing your vector in life. Military writing and frankly that aspect of supervising seemed so transactional to me. The Chief's system is a continuum that categorizes our efforts by aligning those efforts with our resulting impact on our people and our Air Force. The good, the bad, and the ugly all can conform to the Action, Impact, Result model, but without the Chief's system my writing skills lacked direction. This system is a commonsense approach that is ingenious in its simplicity.
>
> —CMSgt Justin Deisch, USAF

Fast forward to the present. While advances in technology make routing blue folders obsolete, the virtual "stack" of performance reports is gone and remains off my desk! I realize this is not the only successful method for writing performance bullets, but over the past decade, these techniques allowed my organizations to be recognized at the highest levels.

In 2012 I came across the strongest report I had ever read. The author offers his thoughts:

> Every bullet I wrote fed the notion . . . to give your best to the people who deserve it. Bullets tend to write themselves when you realize the weight they must bear in a person's career.
>
> The simplest way to craft every bullet is divide them into three distinct parts— What . . . How . . . Result/Impact. Every bullet must begin by answering the question "What did the individual do?" The bullet must inform the reader at the very beginning if the individual was a member/follower in the task, a decision-maker, or a leader/mentor.
>
> The "How" section highlights what was done to accomplish the "What," which introduced the bullet. Numbers identify the accomplishment's magnitude. The first word is often a verb ending with "ed."
>
> Impact can be personnel, unit, base, etc., and may reach all of the way up to the Department of Defense. Numbers are critical here. Money/time/man-hour savings, high percentages achieved, accolades, or low failure/loss rates are all great result/impact descriptors.
>
> In general, put a leadership bullet with far-reaching impact in the most important "top and bottom" lines of your report. Work your way down from there to the member/follower bullet impacts. Hopefully, you will have most, or all, of the space filled up with higher level effects and not have to use the low impact lines at all.
>
> To sum it up, the *magic* of bullet writing starts with the right attitude. Do the right thing for your people . . . they deserve nothing less.
>
> —Lt Col Robert O. Stroebel, USAF, retired

Scoring packages makes you a better writer.

The *magic* is a three-step process that teaches you to read with a critical eye. You will know as you write the bullet how it will be scored and whether that score truly measures the accomplishment. You will also learn what not to write. That is what this book is going to do— teach you to score awards, with the second order effect of making you a more efficient and accomplished writer.

With the genesis of bullet writing *magic* behind us, read on to discover how to build a better mousetrap through line-by-line scoring.

Chapter 2

A Better Mousetrap

Build a better mousetrap, and the world will beat a path to your door.
—Ralph Waldo Emerson

- *Line-by-line scoring prevents halo and horn effects.*
- *Line-by-line scoring saves an incredible amount of time. Interruptions do not impact the outcome.*
- *Score one line at a time for a fair and consistent approach.*
- *Line-item scoring helps resolve tiebreakers; it reveals the strongest and weakest parts of a package.*

This chapter shows the importance of *line-by-line scoring*. Scoring is integral to becoming a better writer. Let's go back a little further to understand how, born out of frustration, this principle built the better mousetrap.

In 1998, as the 15th Air Force C-141 and C-17 aircraft weapons system manager, I had additional duties that included reviewing annual recognition packages. These encompassed everything from individual awards like the Chief Master Sergeant of the Air Force Thomas N. Barnes Crew Chief of the Year to team packages like the Air Force Maintenance Effectiveness Award.

Individual recognition packages were two pages long. With 12 nominees in dozens of categories, the process was labor-intensive and daunting. Nevertheless, individual package work was easy compared to the Maintenance Effectiveness Award. These were 15 pages long, highlighting a year's worth of organizational accomplishments. With four categories ranging from small to large units, there were 30–40 packages to rank.

My first attempt to score 15 pages was a complete disaster. I vividly recall a tall stack hitting my desk for just one category. To top it off, each package was replete with statistics, dollar amounts, time savings, and an unlimited quantity of scientific measurements to compare competing units. One really needed to pay attention.

The initial package took almost all morning. I intently read every line with full attention. When the time came to assign a score, I discovered the guiding instruction only required a value between six and 10 points using half-point increments. Somehow it seemed odd to read hundreds of lines and facts that were then to be boiled down to a single digit between six and ten.

Line-by-line scoring prevents halo and horn effects.

Without reading the other packages, there was no context to which one could relate a score. I had no *feel* for it. I remember wondering what the *right* score should be. It was a pretty solid package and a great effort captured. After much contemplation, I decided to score an "8.5" to establish a baseline.

While this seemed like a good start to the process, it's too easy to feel good or bad about an entire package based on first impressions. Was "8.5" a credible score? If it "seemed" strong from the general positive impression of words or accomplishments, the halo effect can easily give a score too high and unearned. In contrast, one negative bullet may drive the "horn" effect, where the entire package is scored lower. As we will see, line-by-line scoring will prevent these effects.

Line-by-line scoring saves an incredible amount of time.

I picked up a second package but had to stop to attend the weekly staff meeting. Next, a phone call reprioritized my morning and lunch. By the time I resumed, I couldn't recall everything I read on the first two pages and had to make a fresh start. About halfway through again, another phone call and another meeting led to another chance to start over. Time was slipping by. There had to be a better way.

CMSgt Thomas E. Jones, the strategic airlift branch chief, saw my frustration and shared his technique. He showed me how to break the package into small pieces which encouraged a fair and consistent approach.

> As the HH-60 Program Manager in Special Operations Command, the staff scored the major command annual awards. I had some experience; however, like Eric Jaren at Fifteenth Air Force, there was no clear direction or documented process on how to score packages. As a result, there would be different winners amongst board members. With those differences, board members would rescore and if necessary discuss differences. I found in those discussions it was difficult for members to easily support why a particular package was better than another. After relooking at the packages, I would sometimes

notice an accomplishment I did not remember or notice something written as an individual accomplishment with no clear tie to the individual's actions. Bottom line, despite trying my very best, I was not always sure I'd gotten it right. That was unacceptable.

To resolve this, I began using and developing the line-by-line scoring method described in this book for three reasons. One, the scoring of packages would often be interrupted and by scoring each line, I wouldn't be forced to start over. Two, line-by-line scoring put me in a better position to discuss the merits of a package if there wasn't agreement amongst board members. And three, most importantly, it helped to ensure I was selecting the best package.

—CMSgt Thomas E. Jones, USAF, retired

Now it did not matter if I was interrupted. In this system you can resume right where scoring left off without wasted effort. This benefit alone makes the system a better mousetrap. But there's more.

Score one line at a time for a fair and consistent approach.

An added strength of Chief Jones's approach included standardized scoring which assured fairness and consistency. Fairness included removing the halo or horn effects as well as establishing a standard. Consistency thrived in the integrity to a known standard instead of going by "feeling." Bottom line, the scoring system could be trusted.

Chief Jones scored every bullet one line at a time. A strong accomplishment scored half of a point. If an accomplishment impacted beyond the organization, it scored one point. When it made strategic-level impact it scored one and a half points. If the bullet was poorly written, Chief Jones left a goose egg. When finished, he only had to count up the points in the right margin to see which package had the highest score, reflecting the strongest accomplishments. Many number systems work; the important takeaway is to work it line-by-line.

Line scoring helps resolve tiebreakers; it reveals the strongest and weakest parts of a package.

Another benefit of line scoring is tiebreaker resolution. By dividing scores into line-item pieces, board members can refer to their tally in the event of a tie. More importantly, each can justify and discuss in detail why a given score was assigned.

This better mousetrap saved an incredible amount of time. Boards using this process were fair and consistent; system trust was established and secured. Tiebreakers were resolved with confidence. I used this method for three years until the concept was integrated and improved upon in the new scoring program designed for the 715th Air Mobility Squadron. The next chapter builds on the vital necessity for a consistent approach.

Chapter 3

A Consistent Approach

For me the challenge isn't to be different but to be consistent.

—Joan Jett

- *Apply the system fairly and consistently, whether scoring each line up to one point, two points, or by the use of dashes, crosses, or circles.*
- *Different boards can apply a fair and consistent process and arrive at a different outcome.*
- *Remove personal experience that introduces bias and, unintentionally, reeks of the "good-ole boy" system, favoritism, or politics.*
- *Consider the time of day you score. Be sure to score on the same day and at the same time if possible. Changes in rest, nutrition, exercise, and stress can affect consistency.*

Valid results are critical in testing. No matter the scoring system, a consistent approach gives validity and creates a fair result. Line item scoring led the 715th Air Mobility Squadron to a significant time savings and provided fairness. Incorporating this principle also led to better writing through the new awards-scoring seminar.

Our award-scoring seminars gained momentum at the squadron. Early on, only a dozen attended but numbers grew until the conference room was at maximum capacity. Later, people attended even though they weren't participating in a board.

People who struggled to write bullets throughout an entire career suddenly understood.

It was as if a light switch was turned on as they walked out. Feedback was amazing and we kept hearing, "I get it now." Even better, the "scoring seminar" actually revealed writing flaws. Those who struggled to write bullets through an entire career suddenly understood. We were happy as those pesky blue folder stacks *magic*ally disappeared from desks. That's when more *magic* happened.

After teaching the seminar to a majority of our squadron, something very important occurred. The 715th received a disproportionately high number of below-the-zone early promotions, quarterly awards, and annual awards. You can only imagine the impact this had on morale. Within the principles taught in this book is the expectation to perform at a level commensurate with your grade, or above.

The group had four organizations with basically identical missions, composed of the same 20 career specialties. It should be virtually impossible to receive more awards than one or two standard deviations from an equal number of awards. We weren't trying to sweep awards. Supervisors merely composed solid packages that reflected the hard work and contributions of the Airmen serving in their work sections. And 715th Airmen were leading, not just participating. We were managing entire projects, not just supporting the effort.

There was a second order effect as the entire organization stepped up its overall level of performance. In the end, we were building leaders at every level of the organization and documenting the results better than the rest. We were proud, we had spirit, and if you were 7-1-5, you also knew what comes after—"push-ups."

While the overall goal of the seminar and this book is to understand how to evaluate bullet writing and, through that medium, become better at writing, an important underlying tenet is a consistent approach. No matter the scoring rubric, CMSgt Dave Gilmore summed up this principle:

> Lack of standardization is a bad thing and cannot be measured while standardization provides consistency and can be measured.
>
> —CMSgt Dave Gilmore, USAF, retired

Readers need to know that the system presented in this book is not the only one that works. While we were building the seminar, I discovered Chief Sam used a similar technique. He too scored line-by-line, but used symbols instead of numbers.

Whether scoring each line to one point, two points or use dashes, crosses, or circles, apply the system fairly and consistently.

When the chief saw a strong bullet, he marked a dash "-" in the margin. If the accomplishment was significant, he crossed the dash with a "+." When the accomplishment had a strategic level impact he distinguished the line by drawing a circle "0" around the "+." Consistency was the key in this approach. Scores were then tallied to reveal the strongest package.

Board members cannot infer, anticipate, or assume what the individual accomplished. They are charged to read the package. Unfortunately, if an individual's achievement was not documented fully in the recognition package, the accomplishment cannot be fully evaluated. It is not the outcome but the consistent approach that adds integrity to the process. In the final equation, trust matters. So what about applying the board member's personal experience?

Personal experience introduces bias and, unintended, reeks of the good ole' boy system, favoritism, or politics.

Some may argue against a strict line-by-line analysis and favor using "personal experience." Applying this may seem right at the time but will lead down a slippery slope wrought with valid concerns over fairness and bias. You know what they say—perception is reality. A common example is cited by SMSgt Alan Braden:

> As a Career Assistance Advisor, I'm frequently asked to score award packages across the base because I have a broad scope on the installation. Sitting on countless boards, I learned many write to "their audience" instead of the reader. For example, when our Security Forces Airmen emphasize their "TTPs" [techniques, tactics, and procedures] and "BDOC C3" [Base Defense Operations Center, command, control, and communications] plans, I am often scratching my head on how that applies to me. While their efforts are surely impressive, they have forgotten to write to 'their intended audience' which is a medic, bomb loader, etc. . . . You get the picture!
>
> —SMSgt Alan Braden, USAF, retired

Another reason to remove personal experience subjectivity is that it provides no value when a dispute arises. This is critically important, so chapter 10 is dedicated to discussing the need for a fair and consistent dispute process.

Different boards can apply a fair and consistent process and arrive at a different outcome.

To be completely honest we must recognize that people have different values, beliefs, experiences, education, and backgrounds. We do not think the same; the best part about the consistent approach is that it accommodates this diversity. Different boards can apply a consistent process and arrive at different conclusions. When this happens, both conclusions are fair.

Consider the following:

> Board "A" evaluates a set of recognition packages and determines candidate #1 to be the winner. Board "B" follows the same process, but determines candidate #2 to be the winner. Consider the scores between the two packages are within 1/2 of a point, virtually the same score. If both boards used a consistent process, then both boards would be correct and fair in their outcome.

Chief Sam explains his method:

> I normally review my packages at night but the first thing I do is to fold the headings so that the nominee's name is covered. After scoring the packages, I will tally the scores first thing in the morning. On some cases, I have to review the notes I inserted while scoring line by line. The notes clarify or become memory joggers adding the scores in the morning.
>
> —CMSgt Manuel Sarmiento, USAF, retired

While this works for the chief, it may not work for everyone. Strive to score on the same day and at the same time if possible. Changes in rest, nutrition, exercise, and stress can affect consistency. For example, if you are a morning person you may be more generous in the morning and stingy in the evening. It doesn't matter if you are stingy or generous; the scoring curve will be consistent if your evaluation is at the same time of the day.

Both boards applied consistent measurement. Both boards considered every candidate and each one's accomplishments. In following a consistent scoring process, board results are trustworthy. Consistency is practiced by removing personal experience from scoring each accomplishment. These principles assure a fair outcome regardless of the winner.

The first three chapters capture the timeless lessons of bullet writing. We finally understood what we had created. At the end of the day we learned that the seminar taught us to stop writing weak bullet statements. With no more stacks of performance reports and annual award results off the charts, the seminar produced a magical result in creating better writers. There was a second order effect as the entire organization stepped up its overall level of performance. Writers grew superior at evaluating performance and recognizing the accomplishments of people. Giving credit where credit is due and awarding the right people is the cornerstone of recognizing and promoting our greatest asset . . . our Airmen.

> The *Magic of Bullet Writing* is a great tool, foundation, and guideline for any organization. If used and consistently trained to newly assigned members your organization will see an uprising of performance reports, award packages, and even general correspondence going to higher levels, staying and not being sent back for corrections.
>
> —James Shepherd
> Former USAF technical sergeant

The next chapters dig deep into bullet formats and performance levels to fully explain the *magic* of bullet writing.

Part 2

The *Magic*

It is much more difficult to measure nonperformance than performance.

—Harold S. Geneen, American businessman

Part 2 reviews standard bullet formats with an emphasis on linking the tactical, operational, and strategic concepts to the elements in a bullet. Performance levels are discussed, and then demonstration is provided regarding how to use them to interpret degrees of action, impact, and results. Finally, steps are combined to create the *magic*! It's as easy as one, two, three.

The next three chapters will approach writing from a completely different angle. The intent is not to teach you a basic 101-level course on how to write bullet statements. Consider the next three chapters an advanced 301-level course on effective bullet writing.

While this book includes numerous writing tips, the premise is to teach a technique called the "*magic*." The best part—you can apply the *magic* immediately after reading this section.

Chapter 4

Bullet Formats

Small is the number of people who see with their eyes and think with their minds.
—Albert Einstein

- Two- and three-part bullets are essentially the same. Two-part bullets are divided into accomplishment-impact (AI) statements. Three-part bullets, the prevailing bullet format used today, are divided into action-impact-result (AIR) statements.
- The tactical-operational-strategic (TOS) concept connects elements well and explains why some elements do not connect well.
- Bullets can be composed with any part and in any order. Readers typically start at the beginning of the bullet; so, skilled writers position the most important elements at the beginning of the bullet.

Albert Einstein's quote reveals that we see with our eyes what we want to see—without thinking about what we are actually seeing. To help think through bullet writing, we must have a process to do so. This chapter is intended to refresh your memory on the standard bullet formats that are used to write packages, appraisals, and papers. Just as a football team relies on basic plays for its success, the performance writer relies on standard bullet formats to deliver statements that score.

First, we will review the formatting process to make sure we are on the same page. Next will be an introduction to the TOS concept and how it is applied to bullet statements. Finally, examples are given to identify and understand bullet components with the TOS concept.

Bullet Formats

Pick your poison—two-part or three-part bullets. Either one is suitable for communicating accomplishments. Believe it or not, some people get hung up on the precise format of a bullet. Hopefully this chapter will explain how not to get stuck on format and to concentrate on content.

Throughout my career, I honed bullet writing skills by listening to NCOs above me. At Edwards Air Force Base, I was chosen to write the unit's Maintenance Effectiveness Award along with another NCO. In part due to our efforts, the squadron won the Air Force Materiel Command's Maintenance Effectiveness Award for 2005. However, I knew I had a lot more to learn and was always on the lookout for new ways to hone my skills. Flashing forward a few years, I was still at Edwards on the Joint Strike Fighter Program. The base adopted the consistent scoring guidelines outlined in this book. Using those techniques helped me earn one of my Airmen a base level award and also helped write a package for the Ten Outstanding Young Americans for 2010. That Master Sergeant was chosen from hundreds of candidates nationwide to make the final list of 10!

—MSgt Casey T. Schoettmer, USAF, retired

Accomplishment-Impact Format

Air Force Handbook 33-337, *The Tongue and Quill*, illustrated the two-part bullet as the standard format for documenting performance appraisals, recognition packages, and a variety of background papers. These two-part bullets are divided into AI components.

The AI format succinctly documents performance and eliminates unnecessary words that detract from the accomplishment itself. Brevity is the goal. A further examination of the elements is worthwhile.

Accomplishment Element

The *accomplishment* element describes the behavior or *action* of the individual. This critical component describes exactly what the individual did. I cannot stress this enough. A routine mistake made by writers is not stating what the person specifically did. Instead, writers are caught in a trap of ambiguity, which only serves to detract from the accomplishment. You will learn to quickly identify these writing traps in chapter 8.

Impact Element

The *impact* element characterizes the *result* of the behavior. This component is vital to relating relative importance of the action. It gives scope and serves as the connective tissue between the action and the result. The stronger the connection, the stronger the bullet. Later, the TOS concept will explain this strength of connection.

Author's Tip: *The two-part and three-part bullets are essentially the same.*

Please note the emphasized words above. Notice that *Action-Impact-Result* in the two-part description corresponds exactly to the three-part bullet. This shows that both formats are made of essentially the same ingredients.

Action-Impact-Result Format

The prevalent method used today is three parts: Action-Impact-Result. Similar to the two-part bullet, writers are driven to squeeze everything into one line. It is unknown whom to credit for the three-part format, but it now governs as the unofficial standard. It captures what the person did, what the action impacted, and the end result of the action.

Action Element

The action must clearly describe the individual's specific contribution. Without an individual's clear action, you don't have a bullet for which to credit. The action should not only describe the individual's performance but also define the "level" of performance. Did the member perform a task, or was the action performed at a higher level? Ambiguous or unclear statements make it difficult to understand how much value to attribute to the overall accomplishment.

Impact Element

The impact element explains how the individual's performance influenced the next level and provides scope or influence. It also serves as a connector between the action and the result. The stronger the connection between the action and result, the better the bullet. When there is a poor connection, it is difficult to attribute the result to the action.

Result Element

The result qualifies the outcome of the individual's efforts. This becomes the measuring stick and establishes the contribution's value. Tie the results to the big picture. If the results are strategic, then it is important that the impact clearly connects to the individual's efforts. Sometimes writers skip this connection, and the jump to strategic level seems far-fetched. This is the perfect lead in to the Tactical-Operational-Strategic Concept.

Tactical-Operational-Strategic Concept

The TOS concept explains why some elements do or do not connect well. But what are the definitions of TOS levels? Paraphrasing Air Force Doctrine, Volume 2 - Leadership (2015):

> **Tactical Level:** Tactical expertise in the Air Force encompasses chiefly the unit and sub-unit levels where individuals perform specific tasks that, in the aggregate, contribute to the execution of operations at the operational level.
>
> **Operational Level:** At this level, the tactical skills and expertise Airmen developed earlier are employed alongside new leadership opportunities to affect an entire theater or joint operations area.
>
> **Strategic Level:** At this level, an Airman's required competencies transition from the integration of people with missions to leading and directing exceptionally complex and multi-tiered organizations.

The use of TOS highlights faulty writing techniques, such as when a bullet jumps from tactical to strategic. Simply said, it is not likely for tactical-level actions to affect strategic results when the actions do not clearly connect. A strong connection is necessary to receive credit. Without it, many will find zero value and score accordingly. TOS serves as a guide, not a rule.

TOS Model

Figure 1 illustrates a strong bullet with strategic results that connect well to the individual. Notice the bullet moves through each level (action is tactical; impact is operational; and result is strategic). This bullet would have a smooth and logical flow.

> Understanding the TOS model helped me see through "farfetched" bullets when scoring packages. Before learning this I would struggle trying to dissect a bullet and often rendered inappropriate value.
>
> —CMSgt Edward Ames, USAF, retired

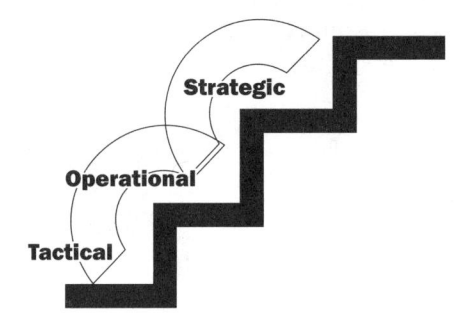

Figure 1. Tactical-Operational-Strategic

Figure 2 illustrates a bullet written at the tactical level. Notice how each component of the bullet is at the tactical level. This bullet would also have a logical flow.

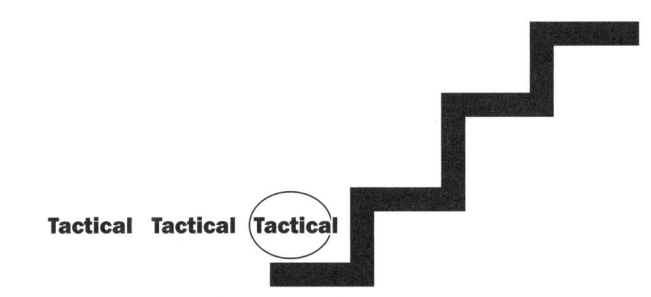

Figure 2. Tactical-Tactical-Tactical

Figure 3 illustrates a bullet written at the operational level. This example also has a logical flow.

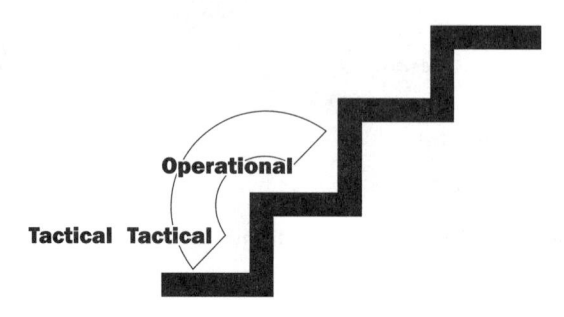

Figure 3. Tactical-Tactical-Operational

Figure 4 is a disconnected bullet. The statement starts at the tactical level, but then it skips to the strategic level. Bullets composed in this format make a poor connection because the contributions of the individual do not connect to the strategic results. TOS explains this as a "bridge too far" for the effort described.

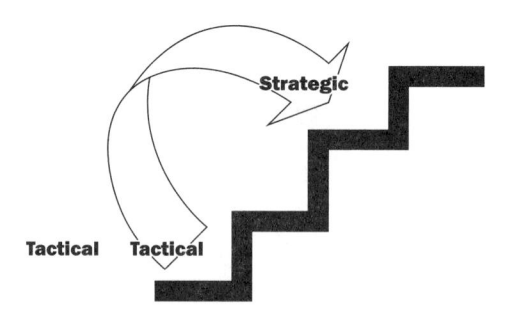

Figure 4. Tactical-Tactical-Strategic

Evaluating TOS

I cannot stress how important it is to describe the connection between levels in the bullet statement. TOS is not something to literally write out, but it is a concept to help understand the congruence of a bullet.

I've seen this TOS issue quite a few times while scoring packages. After seeing a few TOS problems on the same nominee, package credibility was lost. I remember being asked by the board president, a Command Chief, why I scored the package so low. The nominee was a maintainer and a few bullets missed that connection. Another board member, also a maintainer, agreed with my assessment. With line by line scoring and a lack of connection, it was easy to explain my reasoning to the board president.

—CMSgt Manuel Sarmiento, USAF, retired

The example below shows the TOS model at work with example bullets and explanations.

Tactical Element

—**Replaced tire in half job standard**

Tactical

In this example a crew chief changed a tire. The action is clear; so, readers easily recognize the tactical performance.

Operational Element

—**Replaced tire in half job standard; aircraft launched on time**

Tactical   *Operational*

The operational element describes how the individual's actions impacted the mission. The first two elements should unite without confusion. The crew chief changed a tire in half the normally allotted time, which allowed the aircraft to launch on time. The aircraft launch expresses the operational component. This example is very clear.

Strategic Element

—**Replaced tire in half standard; aircraft launched on time— bombs struck target**

Tactical   *Operational*   *Strategic*

The strategic element conveys the wider impact resulting from the action and impact. After launching the aircraft, the jet was able to fulfill its mission of dropping bombs on target contributing to a strategic result. This bullet is a good example of the TOS concept following the tactical-operational-strategic format. The connections are logical from the tactical through strategic spectrum.

The next examples do not connect well.

—**Replaced rivets on cargo door; $2B fleet serviceable—C-5As routed supplies**

    Tactical   *Strategic*   *Strategic*

The tactical accomplishment is clear. The individual changed rivets on a cargo door. The problem is that the strategic level impact and results do not connect to the action. These linkages need to be direct and not casual. Evaluators typically give zero credit for this bullet because it is far-fetched. Information that explains how one individual replacing rivets on one door impacted the entire $2 billion fleet is missing. Additionally, more information is needed to understand how changing rivets led to supplies being delivered by multiple aircraft (in this case it was a fleet C-5As). Bottom line: if the report does not say the individual worked on enough parts for a $2 billion fleet of aircraft, he/she did not. The individual merely replaced rivets on one door, and that is tactical level only.

Fluff

Before going forward, it is critical to introduce another concept. Some call it weak writing; others call it ambiguous writing, but the most common term is fluff. When an accomplishment falls below an expected performance level, this is considered *fluff*, which is not valuable for recognition or merit. Remember at least one component in each bullet must include *action*. Without action, you cannot confirm the individual's presence. Ambiguous action will impact the overall score much more than an ambiguous result. When the word narrative picture begins with fluff, the contribution will not clearly connect to the results. Many will find zero value and score accordingly.

The flowing is an example of fluff:

—**Incredible leader; essential to PERSCO** [personnel support for contingency operations] **team—250 Airmen deployed to AOR** [area of responsibility]

    Fluff   *Fluff*   *Operational*

The *action* and *impact* are fluff, and the reader cannot decipher what the person did. "Incredible leader" does not describe performance. "Essential" is intangible and does not describe impact. Saying they are does not make it so. The only tangible part is the *result*. Unfortunately, the lack of *action* and *impact* prevents the individual from receiving credit for the result.

Here is another example where the lead-in and result are ambiguous.

—**Vital member of team; processed 2K orders—sustained AOR mission**

Fluff   *Operational*   *Fluff*

The important thing to remember about TOS is that members should only be credited for *action*, *impact*, and *result* that can be clearly connected. Do not be influenced by a series of superlatives, adverbs, or other jargon that neglects the actual performance.

Which Format Is Best?

Do not get confused if the bullet does not follow typical formatting. Writers can use a two-part bullet and, at other times, a three-part bullet. Writers will even forgo punctuation marks, and the statement reads more like a complete sentence. Bottom line, bullets can be written in any format, just be sure to know which components are present and identify the value. Regardless of format, remember to capture the interest of the reader.

> To better understand the importance of attracting and keeping the reader's attention, I give you this example: If watching a movie doesn't draw you in by the first 15 minutes, don't [sic] draw you in, most won't continue to watch it. Also, if the movie has you on the edge of your seat throughout, but the ending really stunk, most will not recommend it to a friend. Human nature tells us if we don't attract the evaluator's attention quickly and sustain it, you will not achieve the intended results. So whichever format is best (2-part versus 3-part), I would argue whichever technique achieves this dynamic is the best.
>
> —CMSgt James Martin, USAF, retired

Now let's look at examples of the basic formats to expect.

Example 1: 2-part bullet

—Changed aircraft tire in 1 hour; repair returned aircraft fully mission capable

    Accomplishment   *Impact*

Example 2: 3-part bullet

—Changed aircraft tire; repaired in 1 hour—aircraft fully mission capable

  Action   *Impact*   *Result*

Example 3: Complete sentence

—Changed aircraft tire in 1 hour returning the aircraft to fully mission capable

  Action   *Impact*   *Result*

In the above examples, the same actions and results were recorded and should receive the same value.

Alternative Formats: Reverse or Inverted for Maximum Effect

Conventional wisdom explains the standard techniques should begin with an action element. The ensuing examples illustrate this is not always true.

Example 1: Standard 3-part bullet

—Rewrote technical data; corrected assembly errors—avoided minor wear

  Action   *Impact*   *Result*

This example is a three-part bullet with standard action, impact, and result components. No components are particularly strong, but they are clear. Carefully observe how the structure of the bullet changes depending on the strength of the components.

Example 2: Reverse 3-part bullet

—**Avoided $20M damage! Rewrote technical data; corrected safety errors**

    Result   *Action*   *Impact*

Example 2 is a reverse format. Strong writers move results to the beginning when they are the most significant part of the bullet. Rearranging the bullet ensures the $20 million cost avoidance is not overlooked by the reader. The bottom line—do not bury information. Engineer bullets to help readers clearly see the important parts.

One More Example Set

Example 1: Standard 2-part bullet

—**Rewrote technical data to correct assembly errors; avoided $1.6K wear**

                Accomplishment   *Impact*

Example 2: Reverse 3-part bullet

—**Prevented fleet grounding! Rewrote technical data; avoided $1.6K wear**

    Impact   *Action*   *Result*

In this example, the action and result are not strong but the fleet-wide impact is significant. The bullet was rearranged so the noteworthy part was highlighted at the front.

Putting It All Together

Either two-part or three-part bullets are suitable to effectively communicate performance. Furthermore, bullets can be composed with any part in any order. Skilled writers can position the strongest components at the front of the bullet to strengthen the odds the information will not be overlooked. Engineer the bullet so the most important parts will not be missed. Do not make the reader hunt for the important information. Following these tips will ensure you make the most persuasive environment possible for success.

Chapter 5

Performance Levels

Management is efficiency in climbing the ladder of success; leadership determines whether the ladder is leaning against the right wall.
—Stephen Covey, American businessman/educator

- *Performance levels are not intended to be literal; rather they characterize varying degrees of involvement.*
- *To apply performance levels, look at each piece of the bullet separately and assign a level to that specific component. If the component is weak or ambiguous, assign a lower performance level or call it fluff.*
- *Break down ambiguous components. You must be able to distinguish between those who "walk the walk" from those who only "talk the talk." Determine what the person actually did.*
- *Challenge: select a few bullets from a local award package or performance report. Work with others to evaluate the bullet and compare notes. How did you do?*

Stephen Covey's management and leadership description is very appropriate for this chapter. Performance levels are important for scoring and, in turn, writing. They are defined by interpreting the degree of action, impact, and result corresponding to the level of performance recorded. Performance levels include leadership, management, supervisory, and membership. A nonperformance bullet is called "fluff." This model is a cornerstone of the *magic*.

Performance Levels

Do not confuse *performance levels* with performance. Do not take the definition literally. Instead, use *levels* to characterize varying degrees of action, impact, and result conveyed in the bullet. When reading, you must discern the context of the word in addition to the degree of its characterization.

"As leaders move through successively higher echelons in the Air Force, they need a wider portfolio of competencies," Air Force Doctrine, Volume 2 - Leadership states. Performance levels correlate with the development of Airmen and should reflect the level commensurate with rank and accomplishment. Airmen at the *membership* level reflect performance in competencies needed for their job. At the *supervisory* level, Airmen are expected to perform at a higher level to advance the organization's responsibilities. *Management* and *leadership* skills influence the entire organization and beyond as Airmen continue to advance.

Let me take you back to 2001 to explain the origin of performance levels. Part of the curriculum of the Senior Noncommissioned Officer Academy included a discussion on motivational commitment levels. The exercise included the relevance of three levels—membership, performance, and involvement. The classroom exercise illustrated the higher *performance* and *involvement* levels of activity expected and how to achieve these levels.

I vividly recall the instructor lecturing how senior NCOs should perform at a level of involvement commensurate with their rank and grade. Periodically the instructor would say, "Hey, way to be at membership level" just to drive home the point. This was a way of defining someone who performed a minimal task such as taking out the trash or doing homework.

The point about the performance levels is that you need to document (and perform) above your position or grade. Membership-level performance likely will not separate you from your peers, and if it does, it may separate you the wrong way.

Although there were only three commitment levels described at the academy, I expanded my model to four performance levels due to the importance Air Force Instruction 36-2618, The Enlisted Force Structure, places on continuing to develop leadership and management skills. Four levels—membership, supervisory, management, and leadership—present a model that corresponds well to rank structures.

> Four levels—membership, supervisory, management, and leadership—present a model that corresponds well to rank structures.

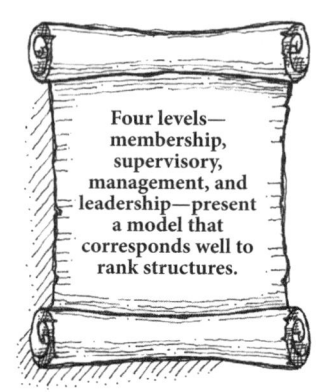

Performance Model

Figure 5 expresses the performance-level model. In broad brush terms, it reflects how you can go from floor sweeper to the boss. Although the portrayal revolves around the military, the premise can be universally applied to any system. Each step in the ladder reflects increased responsibility, and, more important, increased expectation.

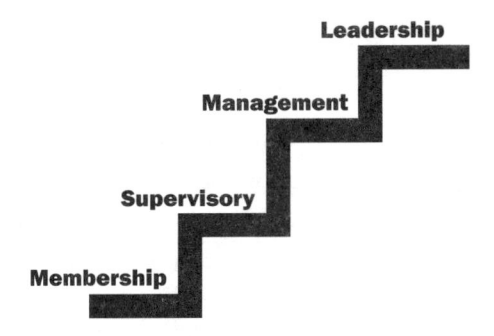

Figure 5. Performance-level model

Membership defines the apprentice to journeyman and the junior ranks. The supervisory level includes journeymen, supervisors, and NCOs. Management comprises craftsmen and senior NCOs. Lastly, and this can be difficult contextually, the leadership level describes the contribution that anyone can perform well above expectations. Similar to ambiguous writing, if an accomplishment is below an expected performance level, is it worth documenting on the performance report or recognition package? The principle behind performance levels is not what you are capable of but what is expected.

> I like to use the crawl-walk-run example when explaining each performance level. The question must be asked, "what am I being asked to do"? When performing at the membership level, I'm being asked to crawl, at the supervisory level we walk, at the management level we jog, and at the leadership level we are running.
> —CMSgt Wesley Riopel, USAF, retired

Performance Definitions

The following are basic definitions of performance levels. Please do not get caught up in literal definitions. Levels are used incrementally to denote various degrees of action, impact, and results.

Membership

Membership-level performance infers tactical-level activities on a small scale. These actions are the building blocks toward larger accomplishments. These efforts depict contributions of a junior Airman, an apprentice, or the expected daily tasking of someone higher ranked:

- Job performance in your primary duty includes helping, assisting, participating, and supporting.
- Self-improvement describes short training courses, college classes, exams like the College-Level Examination Program (CLEP)—things that would be considered the building blocks toward more significant educational accomplishments.
- Base and community involvement includes helping, assisting, participating, and supporting.
- Mentoring includes your impact on the people in your charge.

Supervisory

Supervisory-level performance is tactical or operational in nature. These efforts depict actions normally accomplished by NCOs or journeymen:

- Job performance includes oversight or supervision of a small group, small team, or small program and taking charge of tactical activities.
- Self-improvement describes short in-residence or correspondence courses or certifications and completion of career development courses, and completion of the Community College of the Air Force (CCAF) degree.
- Base and community involvement includes oversight or supervision of small groups or small teams and organizing/leading small-scale base and community activities.
- Mentoring includes impact on the Airmen in your charge and expansion to those around you.

Management

Management-level is more operational in nature. These efforts depict activities normally accomplished by senior NCOs or craftsmen:

- Job performance includes leading multiple teams, multiple programs, and/or large populations and organizing, directing, planning, and controlling large-scale projects.
- Self-improvement efforts describe significant educational and training milestones, long in-residence or correspondence courses, career development course completion with outstanding grades and distinction, and completion of undergraduate degrees.
- Base and community involvement includes leading multiple teams, multiple programs, and/or large populations and organizing, directing, planning, and controlling large-scale projects.
- Mentoring at the management level depicts activities with influence over large groups of Airmen inside and outside the organization and significant involvement in professional development.

Leadership

Leadership-level performance depicts strategic involvement. These are functions expected from a leader. Remember, anyone has the potential to perform at the leadership level:

- Job performance verbiage includes organizing, directing, planning, and supervising large programs and/or vast populations and assuming responsibility over major operations.
- Self-improvement describes higher-level educational achievements and/or significant in-residence courses and completion of graduate degrees.
- Base and community involvement includes organizing, directing, planning, and supervising large base and community programs, overseeing vast operations, and assuming responsibility over vast populations.
- Mentoring in this category demonstrates influence over hundreds of Airmen throughout the base and involvement organizing professional development panels and seminars. These leaders offer comments at graduations and other professional development venues.

Context

While anyone can demonstrate leadership, a certain level of performance is expected based on your rank or position. Therefore, you should be performing at a level commensurate with or above your position.

Often the context of a word matters more than the word itself. For example, look at the word *leader* in this bullet: "Leader! Washed cars for the booster club." This is fluff and should hold no value. The word is inappropriately used to influence the reader. After all, the individual only washed cars, which is membership level at best.

Conversely, a *member* of the USAF Uniform Board should carry great value. Not many people will ever have the opportunity to participate on the USAF Uniform Board, where they can affect Air Force-wide change.

Bottom line: Do not get caught in a trap placing a stigma on the definition of a word—look for context.

Apply Performance Levels to Bullets

Chapter 4 evaluated how bullets can be constructed in standard, reverse, and inverted formats. Bullets were also divided into pieces, giving insight into the writer's communication style. As an evaluator, you need to assign the appropriate level to each specific bullet component. If the performance is strong, assign a higher performance level. If the component is weak or ambiguous, assign a lower performance level or call it fluff.

Consider the following example: "Hard-charging attitude and dedication directly contributed to the unit winning the Air Force Verne Orr Award." The result seems to be leadership-level since the award was won at the Air Force level. However, "hard-charging attitude and dedication" are vague words and add no value. This fluff limits credibility and hinders any bullet potential.

Upper and Lower Thresholds

One technique to assist in assigning a performance level is to find upper and lower thresholds for a particular accomplishment. For example, an individual who instructed leadership principles to 25 students during a one-day course might be considered leadership level. Leadership is demonstrated at any rank and is performed at the tactical, operational, and strategic levels. However, first consider the realistic and achievable possibilities for mentoring.

In trying to estimate what level of performance to assign, imagine what other mentors are accomplishing. What about the individuals who organized the following:

- Taught two subordinates how to write performance reports;
- Instructed 25 students on leadership principles during a one-day course;
- Organized weeklong senior noncommissioned officer professional development seminar for 50 in conjunction with a banquet dinner;
- Taught two professional enhancement (PE) seminars, three Airmen Leadership Schools (ALS), three First-Term Airmen Center (FTAC), and organized a tour for the Reserve Officer Training Corps (ROTC), shaping 350 future leaders.

By establishing realistic upper and lower thresholds you can compare and contrast an appropriate level of performance. In this case, what could have been perceived as leadership-level mentoring in the first two bullets falls short when compared to organizing a senior NCO professional development seminar and completely pales by comparison to the person involved in the yearlong shaping of 350 future leaders. Now the original accomplishment appears more like it corresponds to supervisory level—"oversight or supervision of a small group, small team, small program." The others should appear more like membership, management, and leadership level, respectively.

The reason to mention these thresholds stems from evaluators who profess to grade on a curve. Some purport a junior Airman organizing a car wash demonstrates leadership and thus award credit at the leadership level. Doing this only serves to diminish the contributions of other Airmen performing at a higher level. What about the president of the Airman's Council who leads a yearlong committee, conducts monthly meetings, and meets with base leadership regularly? That is leadership level. Organizing a car wash is supervisory level (oversight of a small group), and in my opinion, such effort should not be graded on a curve. As you can see, applying proper context helps you to identify the performance for what it is and be confident in your choice.

Two-Levels Concept

There will never be a perfect system to score bullets, because you cannot apply a checklist system to people's values, backgrounds, experience, or interpretation of the intended message. However, you can apply the two-levels concept. When evaluating a bullet select "two" adjacent performance levels with the confidence you have the right choice between the two levels. For example, if a person performed a certain accomplishment resulting in a $2,000,000 savings, that should be considered a leadership-level result.

By applying the two-levels concept, practically every person should agree that a $2,000,000 result is either a leadership or a management level. That's a lot of money! It should be unusual to believe a $2,000,000 result would be membership level. Every evaluator should be within one level of each other by applying the two-levels concept.

The two-levels concept validates how two board members should not be off by more than one level. For example, if one board member thought the accomplishment is membership, it should be difficult for another to perceive it as leadership. Any two board members usually fall within one level of each other. If someone falls outside one level repeatedly, they are often inexperienced, occasionally parochial, or may have a unique perspective falling outside the norm. I say the last part to give flexibility for unique and diverse thoughts, but in all honesty, in 14 years of using this process, everyone who fell outside the two levels was one of the first two reasons.

In addition, if you find yourself having difficulties deciding on a specific level, try using the two-levels concept. Selecting two levels will help you find the range. Once you are in the range, try to determine what your next choice would be. Is it one up or one down from your two levels? For example, if you selected management and supervisory for the two levels, does the accomplishment seem more like leadership or membership? If your next choice was membership, then your specific performance level is probably supervisory. The two-levels concept helps you pinpoint performance levels.

Summary

By now, you should be able to differentiate levels of performance. Also, you should be able to distinguish different bullet formats and recognize strengths and weaknesses in bullet components. In all jobs, some people "help" and some "lead." Leadership can happen at any level, and consideration must be given to the person's rank and position to understand which accomplishments are meaningful and worthy of documenting and which ones are not.

Chapter 6

The Performance Scale

If it's free, it's advice; if you pay for it, it's counseling; if you can use either one, it's a miracle.
  —Jack Adams, coach and general manager, Detroit Red Wings

The *magic* is a three-step process. First, assess the bullet format. Next, assign a performance level to each part of the bullet. Finally, determine the overall level of the accomplishment.

- *Remember how to apply the two levels concept. By understanding this concept, everyone should be within one level of each other.*
- *Accommodate imperfection by considering the two levels concept; board members should conclude within one level of each other.*
- *Challenge: If the examples seemed difficult, practice by considering the scores of an experienced evaluator on an award package.*

This short chapter brings all the pieces together. The *magic* is not a miracle, it is a process—a process to save time and make writing easier and stronger. Learning how to assess bullet formats and performance levels is the foundation for this process. This chapter creates the *magic* by combining key lessons learned in previous chapters and establishing an overall performance level. Now it is time for the *magic*.

Performance Scale

Chapter 4 showed how to break apart and assess the strengths and weaknesses of the bullet format. Chapter 5 assigned performance levels to each part of the bullet. Chapter 6 combines the first two steps to determine the overall level of the accomplishment through the use of the Performance Scale.

Over the years, I have used a variety of scales and graphs to illustrate performance levels. This process has evolved considerably and you will be glad to see how the performance scale brings it all together. The Performance Scale arranges the components and illustrates the strengths and weaknesses within the bullet.

As you read a bullet, start by identifying the construction and format and then assess the performance levels in each element. Based on the overall assessment of the bullet, assign and write that performance level in the right-hand column. It seems simple; that is the *magic*.

Use the scale to visualize each component with the corresponding level of performance inside the chart.

Performance Scale Example

—Negotiated MOA; raised aircraft ramp space 25%—facilitated beddown of aircraft

	Action	Impact	Result
Leadership	—	—	—
Management	**Negotiated MOA**	—	—
Supervisory	—	raised aircraft ramp space 25%	facilitated beddown...
Membership	—	—	—
Fluff	—	—	—

In the preceding example, the *action* is the strongest part at management level, the *impact* is supervisory, and the *result* is supervisory. For the purposes of this book we will use this chart. Afterwards, you will automatically visualize bullet components to see the strengths and weaknesses as if they were placed in the chart.

Practice

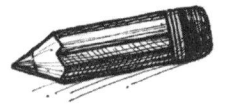

As you review the following examples think about what performance levels you would assign. Then read the rationale. Remember to consider upper and lower thresholds. Are we close?

Example 1

Standard Bullet Format

—Changed aircraft tire; completed in 1 hour—aircraft mission capable

	Action	Impact	Result
Leadership	—	—	—
Management	—	—	—
Supervisory	—	—	—
Membership	Changed aircraft tire	completed in 1 hour	aircraft mission...
Fluff	—	—	—

Example 1 reflects all of the components at the membership level. A crew chief changed an aircraft tire. The job was completed within the standard, and the aircraft was returned to serviceable status. This is a basic task for a crew chief, and the performance scale portrays the accomplishment at membership level.

Example 2

Standard Bullet Format

—Rewrote technical data; corrected assembly errors—averted minor wear

	Action	Impact	Result
Leadership	—	—	—
Management	—	—	—
Supervisory	Rewrote technical data; corrected assembly errors		
Membership	—	—	averted minor wear
Fluff	—	—	—

Example 2 graphically illustrates how some elements in the bullet are at different performance levels. The result offers no tangible information. If I had to select a level other than membership for the result, it would be fluff. This system is not a perfect science; however, your evaluation of the components in this accomplishment should be within one level as shown.

Example 3

Reverse Bullet Format

—Avoided $20M damage! Rewrote technical data to avoid catastrophic damage

	Accomplishment	Impact
Leadership	Avoided $20M damage!	—
Management	—	—
Supervisory	—	Rewrote technical data to avoid catastrophic errors
Membership	—	—
Fluff	—	—

Example 3 uses the reverse format to position the $20 million damage to the front of the bullet and emphasize the significance. Most readers would probably agree that "Avoided $20M damage" is at the leadership or management level. Rewriting technical data is supervisory, and the end of the bullet is ambiguous, leaving it scored membership. It possibly should be fluff.

Example 4

Inverted Bullet Format

—Corrected fleet-wide issue! Rewrote technical data to prevent minor wear

	Impact	Action	Result
Leadership	—	—	—
Management	Corrected flee-wide...	—	—
Supervisory	—	Rewrote technical data	—
Membership	—	—	to prevent minor wear
Fluff	—	—	—

Example 4 uses the inverted format to move the fleet-wide impact to the front. Avoiding minor wear was not significant; rewriting technical data is not the strongest part of the bullet. The performance scale illustrates how this bullet started strong, but fell off at the end. This would be better than starting weak.

So far, the examples are relatively straightforward, which is not what one should expect when scoring awards. Moreover, we often score awards outside our field of expertise. This can be tough unless the action, impact, and results are clear. The next four examples include ambiguous writing to make you break down the bullet and eliminate ambiguity to find value. Hours are spent rewriting bullets that look just like these.

Example 5

Reverse Bullet Format

—Won AF Safety plaque! Led effort resulting in zero unit safety issues

	Result	*Action*	*Impact*
Leadership	Won AF Safety plaque!	—	—
Management	—	—	—
Supervisory	—	—	—
Membership	—	—	resulting in zero unit safety issues
Fluff	—	Led effort	—

The writer used a reverse format to emphasize an Air Force-level award. Sadly, this bullet falls into a writing trap as it does not describe anything tangible performed by the individual. Writing traps will be examined later on in chapter 8. The lack of tangible action results in overall little or no value. The performance scale makes the ambiguous contribution readily apparent.

Example 6

Standard Bullet Format

—Selfless leader! Co-led fundraiser to raise money for unit holiday party

44 | JAREN

	Action	Impact	Result
Leadership	—	—	—
Management	—	—	—
Supervisory	—	—	—
Membership	—	Co-led fundraiser to raise money for unit holiday party	
Fluff	Selfless leader!	—	—

Example 6 is filled with ambiguity. The beginning is fluff, and leading a small fundraiser should be at the supervisory level. Unfortunately, the writer does not say what the person did. Summing up the three components, it is fluff-membership-fluff. With added information the bullet could be valued overall at the supervisory level. As presented, I would probably award overall membership or fluff. Make sense? The performance scale clearly exposes this bullet as a membership level contribution at best.

An old adage exemplifies this situation. *If a tree fell in the forest and no one was there to see it, did it really happen? If the bullet does not say what they did, do not give credit for it. It did not really happen.*

Example 7

Standard Bullet Format

—Managed flight CFC [Combined Federal Campaign] **drive; installation surpassed FY11 goal raising $1.1M**

	Accomplishment	Impact
Leadership	—	**installation surpassed FY11 goal raising $1.1M**
Management	—	—
Supervisory	—	—
Membership	**Managed flight CFC drive**	—
Fluff	—	—

The bullet in example 7 claims flight management of the effort but offers no scope, impact, or contribution details. The beginning of the bullet becomes a management-level job description that is not backed up with action. This could have been a good bullet if it described management-level information such as the population in the flight, the percent of people contacted, and dollar value raised. Applying the TOS concept, this bullet jumps from tactical to strategic without connection.

Example 8

Standard Bullet Format

—Astute fiscal manager; maintained perfect records—office aced IG inspection

	Action	Impact	Result
Leadership	—	—	—
Management	—	—	office aced IG inspection
Supervisory	—	—	—
Membership	—	maintained perfect records	—
Fluff	Astute fiscal manager	—	—

Example 8 is another example of ambiguous language. The problem is the action and impact. What were the astute actions? Why were the records flawless? Did they initiate a new process or does the computer system automatically maintain flawless records and there was no action? The writer should cite clearly what the person did to distinguish between those who "walk the walk" from those who only "talk the talk."

> Another rule of thumb in describing fluff is where the writer states the individual is "all that" but doesn't back it up in the bullet. Simply saying someone is good doesn't make it so. Instead, avoid the fluff and simply talk to the performance (and do so convincingly) so the reader is able to draw that conclusion without using the words "all that." Following this strategy empowers you with a powerful performance-based writing technique which is the essence of persuasion. Do not just "tell me" they are an astute fiscal manager, "Show me!"
>
> —CMSgt James Martin, USAF, retired

For example, if each component (action, impact, and result) is membership value (membership-membership-membership), it is easy to see how the entire bullet is scored membership level. The same is true if each component is assigned supervisory value (supervisory-supervisory-supervisory). The entire bullet would be scored supervisory level. It gets trickier when components have varying performance levels (membership-leadership-supervisory). Identify the components, assign a performance level, and then determine the overall bullet value.

A good technique to assess performance is to underline the words that stand out particularly strong and circle the words that are ambiguous, unclear, or weak. Then make notes in the right-hand margin.

Practice

The following three examples are designed to practice assessing bullets. Evaluate the statement and assign one performance level to each component. Using a pencil write the bullet components adjacent to the corresponding performance level. Then, turn the page and compare your assessment. Also, remember the two levels concept. Your estimation does not have to match perfectly, but see if it is within one level.

Example 1 (Practice)

—Replaced worn tires; completed task in one hour—vehicle returned to service

	Action	Impact	Result
Leadership	—	—	—
Management	—	—	—
Supervisory	—	—	—
Membership	—	—	—
Fluff	—	—	—

Author's Tip: Remember, a scoring process is not a perfect science. A checklist is not available for assessing bullets because individual values and experiences differ from person to person and affect evaluations when making assessments.

Example 1 (Author's)

— Replaced worn tires; completed task in one hour—vehicle returned to service

	Action	Impact	Result
Leadership	—	—	—
Management	—	—	—
Supervisory	—	—	—
Membership	Replaced worn tires; completed in one hour—vehicle returned...		
Fluff	—	—	—

Membership level best describes this accomplishment. A maintenance person replaced worn tires on a vehicle. Completing the task in one hour and returning the vehicle to service are direct outcomes from the tire change. Though the task was completed in one hour, it still represents a basic task that "members" do—nothing more and nothing less. What if the task were completed in one-half the job standard? Can you see how that might affect your assessment?

Author's Tip: *Typically, board members do not have perfectly matching scores. However, it is unusual for one person to believe an action is membership level while another person considers it leadership.*

Example 2 (Practice)

— Replaced aircraft tire on Redball—quick repair allowed successful exercise

	Accomplishment	Impact
Leadership	—	—
Management	—	—
Supervisory	—	—
Membership	—	—
Fluff	—	—

Author's Tip: *"Redball" is common in aircraft maintenance. It signifies a problem in the final moments before taxi. Typically, the aircraft has engines running. This creates intensity for repair actions.*

Example 2 (Author's)

—Replaced aircraft tire on Redball—quick repair allowed successful exercise

	Accomplishment	Impact
Leadership	—	—
Management	—	—
Supervisory	Replaced tire on Redball—quick repair allowed successful...	
Membership	—	—
Fluff	—	—

Although the crew chief only changed a tire, the intensity of the Redball increased the significance of the accomplishment. Also, the aircraft actually launched and participated in an exercise after maintenance.

Author's Tip: *This bullet describes competencies expected of skilled workers, a level expected from a craftsman.*

Also, though "Redball" is now explained, this term can be ambiguous for nonaircraft maintenance board members. Consider the audience when writing the bullet.

Example 3 (Practice)

—Replaced aircraft tire on Redball; last jet for CAS [close air support]—2 bombs hit targets

	Action	Impact	Result
Leadership	—	—	—
Management	—	—	—
Supervisory	—	—	—
Membership	—	—	—
Fluff	—	—	—

Author's Tip: *The intensity and situation continue to add value. Imagine trying to repair the last jet available to ensure our war fighters have close air support.*

Example 3 (Author's)

—Replaced aircraft tire on Redball; last jet for CAS—2 bombs hit targets

	Action	Impact	Result
Leadership	—	—	2 bombs hit targets
Management	—	last jet for CAS	—
Supervisory	Replaced aircraft tire on Redball	—	—
Membership	—	—	—
Fluff	—	—	—

Management level best describes this accomplishment. Applying the two-level rule, most readers will score the accomplishment as management or leadership due to the intensity and significance of the result.

> *Author's Tip*: Interestingly in the three examples, the only thing accomplished by the worker is a tire change. This example makes it obvious that pertinent details, such as the last jet, last-minute tire change, and enabling the jet to strike targets are essential ingredients. With a clear scenario description, the overall value of the contribution changes significantly.

Summary

So how did you do? Were you within one level? The three step process to assess every bullet with a performance level is essential to applying the *magic*. If you're still a little rusty, the following chapters and online practice at http://www.brownbaglessons.com/ will continue to build skills by practicing the line-by-line scoring system. In addition, readers will discover important writing traps to avoid.

Board members are charged to evaluate the individual's contributions against the competencies in the recognition criteria. After reading this chapter you should have a solid technique to guide you in evaluating bullets. Whether writing for the board or evaluating packages on the board, composing input to submit for consideration in your annual appraisal or your résumé, your results will be credible and defendable.

Part 3

Practice Makes Perfect

In theory, there is no difference between theory and practice. But, in practice, there is.

—Yogi Berra, baseball professional

Practice makes perfect. Or does it? If someone writes bullets for 20 years, should not that person be a perfect bullet writer? Experience shows this is certainly not the case. So what kind of practice makes perfect?

Part 3 gets back to the basics. When a professional sports team struggles, the coach drills the team on basic mechanics. Coach John Wooden was the head coach of the University of California–Los Angeles (UCLA) men's basketball team from 1964 to 1975. The team won 10 national titles under his leadership. Coach Wooden used a famous lesson on shoes and socks to explain the importance of getting back to the basics. He taught his players to properly wear and tie footgear to prevent blisters that might take them out of the game. Basics are usually enough to get performance back on track.

After "creating" the *magic*, chapter 7 hones the basics with a practice of scoring mechanics. An advanced coaching technique involves practicing specific activities to remove flaws engrained from years of bad habits. This chapter accomplishes this by identifying common writing traps to avoid.

Finally, there are peak performance team practice examples that show how the excellent mechanics become a natural reflex. The following exercise will build this adaptive response by providing examples to practice and compare your results to the author's rationale. Let's practice!

Chapter 7

Scoring Mechanics

Do not measure yourself by what you have accomplished, but what you should have accomplished with your ability.

—John Wooden, collegiate basketball coach

- Practice doesn't make perfect, "perfect practice makes perfect."
- Line-by-line scoring is essential to remove bias and this method ensures that it is an objective, fair, and consistent process.
- Read a bullet from left to right. Underline the elements you find particularly strong and circle the elements that you find ambiguous, unclear, or weak. Read, underline, circle, then score in the right margin.
- The bottom line—work the scoring mechanics. Let the process work, let the process be fair, and let objectivity be your compass.

By this point, the reader has an understanding of formats, performance levels, and creating the *magic*. Now it is time to practice the process.

K. Anders Ericsson, a psychologist and professor at Florida State University, pioneered research in deliberate practice and what deliberate practice means. One of Ericsson's core findings is that how expertly a skill is performed has more to do with *how* the practitioner practices rather than with the *repetition* of that skill.[1] A typical coaching technique is to break down the skills that are required to improve an athlete's performance and focus on specific aspects during practice or day-to-day activities.

This is why the method (the *how*) of practicing scoring mechanics develops your evaluation ability. This chapter contains a practice page and the author's corresponding appraisal to compare your efforts. First let's set up the practice.

Tenets of Scoring Mechanics

- Score one line at a time without regard to other lines
- Start by reading the bullet from left to right

- Identify components: accomplishment-impact, action-impact-result
- Underline components you find particularly strong
- Circle components you find ambiguous, unclear, or weak
- Consider performance levels that best describe the components
- At the end of the bullet, consider the performance level that best characterizes the overall accomplishment
- Place a score from zero to two points (see table 1) in the right margin that corresponds to the overall level of performance
- Score every single bullet until all have a score in the right margin

Table 1. Performance-level scores

Leadership	2 points
Management	1 1/2 points
Supervisory	1 point
Membership	1/2 point
Fluff	0 point

Author's Tip: Remember at least one component in each bullet must include action. Without action, you cannot confirm the individual was even present. Ambiguous action will negatively impact the overall value much more than an ambiguous result.

Scoring awards is not supposed to be subjective, nor about the person you like. It is also not about the personal "experience" of a seasoned leader making judgments. It's about being objective, fair, and consistent.

Line-by-Line Scoring Is a Powerful Tool

The truth is every board member has bias, preference, values, and personal views that can interfere in the scoring process. Everyone has these subconscious influences, but a line-by-line evaluation helps to overcome personal bias. Let me share one of my own examples:

On one occasion while preparing to score packages, I recognized one of the candidates had just returned from a deployment (let's call this package A). That deployment was filled with incredible adventure and opportunity. In the back of my mind, something told me this person would come out on top.

During the scoring process, several of his accomplishments jumped out at me. Following the techniques in this book, I underlined the strong accomplishments, circled the weak, and scored in the margin.

Using this system, you can understand the difficulty of demonstrating leadership-level performance on every line. The level of these accomplishments is enduring, significant, and not easy to achieve. Package A had a few 2s denoting leadership-level contributions as well as a number of management- and supervisory-level accomplishments. Then I scored the remaining packages. When finished, I tallied up the scores. I can't remember the actual point value; let's say package A scored 40 points. Forty points is a good score using this system for a package with 30 lines. My intuition led me to believe that that package would end up winning.

However, after tallying the scores, it surprised me to learn that package B scored 43 points which resulted in my number one recommendation. In the back of my mind, that just did not add up. How could my intuition be wrong?

I reviewed the scores on both packages line-by-line to double-check strengths and weaknesses and came up with same result. Then the clue light came on. Through objective line-by-line scoring, the record of accomplishment clearly showed package B to be the stronger package. If I had allowed my bias to influence scoring, package A would have incorrectly been selected as the winner.

I stand by the benefits of a consistent approach because this process leads to a fair outcome, certainly a fairer outcome than a personal preference method. Combining the *magic* with line-by-line scoring and proper scoring mechanics compensates for internal bias and recognizes the merit of individual accomplishments. What an incredible discovery!

Practice

Example 1 represents a typical awards package. Your task is to score each bullet. Begin by scanning each line left to right assessing the various components (action, impact, and result). While reading, underline the parts you consider strengths and circle the parts you consider weaknesses. Then consider your performance level assessment for each component and write the score (between zero and two points) that best summarizes the overall level of the accomplishment in the right margin. Be mindful these bullets are shortened to fit the width of the page. When you are finished, compare your assessment to that provided by the author in example 2.

You will achieve the best benefit by scoring the example package before comparing it against the author. Now let's begin.

Example 1

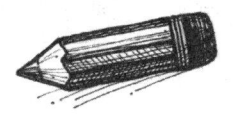

Leadership and Job Performance in Primary Duties

Leader! Updated fitness tracker—current stats 100% compliant	__ pts.
Led inspection review; validated 13 checklists/350 items—passed UCI	__ pts.
Dedication helped the unit win the Air Force Outstanding Unit Award	__ pts.
Revised training; saved 15 hours/person—affected 10K employees	__ pts.
ORM practices instrumental to unit's nom of CSAF Ground Safety Award	__ pts.

Self-Improvement

Completed 16 credits toward bachelor's degree—maintained 3.6 GPA	__ pts.
Hard Charger! Completed 12 CBTs—100% compliant with mobility trng	__ pts.

Base and Community Involvement

Facilitated 5-day seminar; guided 24 speakers—developed 63 SNCOs	__ pts.
Mentor! Taught 3 schools, 2 seminars, 5 courses—shaped 399 juniors	__ pts.
Built Professional Development program; elevated employee abilities	__ pts.

Now compare your results to Example 2 which has been filled in with the author's appraisal. Did the components you underlined and circled correspond? Remember the two levels concept; did the score you placed in the right-hand margin come within one level of the scores provided by the author?

Example 2

Leadership and Job Performance in Primary Duties

Leader! Updated fitness tracker—current stats 100% compliant	0.5 pts.
Led inspection review; validated 13 checklists/350 items—passed UCI	1.0 pts.
Dedication helped the unit win the Air Force Outstanding Unit Award	0.5 pts.
Revised training; saved 15 hours/person—affected 10K employees	1.5 pts.
ORM practices instrumental to unit's nom of CSAF Ground Safety Award	0.5 pts.

Self-Improvement

Completed 16 credits toward bachelor's degree—maintained 3.6 GPA	1.0 pts.
Hard Charger! Completed 12 CBTs—100% compliant with mobility trng	0.5 pts.

Base and Community Involvement

Facilitated 5-day seminar; guided 24 speakers—developed 63 SNCOs	1.5 pts.
Mentor! Taught 3 schools, 2 seminars, 5 courses—shaped 399 juniors	2.0 pts.
Built Professional Development program; elevated employee abilities	0.5 pts.

A Final Look

A good technique before you finish scoring is to review packages side-by-side to spot discrepancies. Maybe you scored earning an associate's degree 1.5 points in one package, but 1.0 point in another. This added step ensures fairness and consistency among packages.

The Human Factor

Though line-by-line scoring minimizes bias, the "human factor" cannot be ignored. One cannot ignore the dynamic that it is impossible for complete objectivity from thoughts, feelings, and emotions. They are, in fact, part of the scoring process. You must be mindful of this. Chief James Martin explains:

> An evaluator proceeded to use the scoring method discussed. When finished, the winning package scored 9.5 and the second scored 9.0. If you have experi-

ence scoring packages you know it is common for the difference between winners and second place to be a mere half-point.

Hypothetically, it's safe to conclude a package scoring 9.5 points out of a possible 10 is very strong. But the same argument can be made for the 9.0 package. After all, it's only a half-point away from first place. Asking the evaluator, "how did you score the difference," you will come to the conclusion I did many years ago. Though both packages are good, one package impressed the board member more. Whether it's the entire package or one or two bullets, it was the persuasive factor that made the difference. I call it the "wow" factor. You must account for that and incorporate this into your writing. It's an important dynamic you can't overlook. Use this as you create the magic.

—CMSgt James Martin, USAF, retired

Formula for Success

In my bullet-writing presentation, I present an emerging thought on the bullet value and the formula for success. The *action* establishes the "potential value" of the bullet, then the *result* component "qualifies" the accomplishment. You must have both, but in my opinion, a bullet starting at the membership level limits the potential of the bullet. However, if the action component is the leadership level, the potential of the bullet will continue to increase commensurate with the level of the result component.

Summary

A person can write for years and never improve. Then along comes a mentor, a coach, or an approach that radically improves the writer's product immediately. Apply this chapter's scoring process and the *magic* takes root and comes alive in your writing. Now you are better able to detect the strengths and weaknesses of your and others' writing. By applying these techniques, you will be leaps and bounds ahead of others.

The bottom line is to work the process, then let the process work. Minimize bias, and let objectivity be your compass. When you do, the process will be fair, consistent, and objective.

Chapter 8

Top 10 Writing Traps

There are three types of lies—lies, damn lies, and statistics.
—Mark Twain

☐ *Be sure you can recognize the various writing traps:*

1. Making promises
2. Faulty lead-in
3. Led effort
4. Job title
5. Death bullet
6. Lazy writing
7. Too many acronyms
8. Bridge too far
9. Know your audience
10. Who's your audience

> **Author's Tip**: You should not expect to find perfect packages when scoring awards. However, don't disregard an entire bullet just because you recognize a portion contains fluff. There may be enough information remaining to find some value.

Continuing with the notion that perfect practice makes perfect, whatever sport one plays, bad habits will follow throughout life unless you identify and correct those habits by practicing proper form or technique. This chapter presents 10 examples of the most-common writing traps. Every example is designed to help identify the flaws that detract from performance appraisals, recognition packages, résumés, and other professional reports.

Unfortunately, the wool has been pulled over our eyes through repetitive bad habits. Learn these common writing traps and your eyes will be opened to the prevalent flaws found across the spectrum.

This chapter presents essential tips to improve your abilities. As you read the examples continue to look for format, performance levels, and value. The flaws will become apparent as the performance scale amplifies the strengths and weaknesses.

Example 1: The "making promises" trap

—Studying for College Math CLEP exam; expect six credits towards associate's degree

	Accomplishment	Impact
Leadership	—	—
Management	—	—
Supervisory	—	—
Membership	—	—
Fluff	Studying for College Math CLEP exam; expect six credits towards...	

<u>Zero points—fluff; fluff–fluff</u>. This bullet attempts to take credit for something that has not happened.

> *Author's Tip*: How can you confirm an individual is truly studying for a CLEP? It's not a college class which requires enrollment. This bullet is promising on something yet to occur. Avoid the making promises trap.

Example 2: The "faulty lead-in" trap

—Hard Charger! Completed 12 CBTs—100% current with mobility training

	Action	Impact	Result
Leadership	—	—	—
Management	—	—	—
Supervisory	—	—	—
Membership	— Completed 12 CBTs—100% current with mobility training		
Fluff	Hard Charger!	—	—

<u>1/2 point–fluff; membership–membership</u>. Using the lead-in "hard charger" is an ambiguous beginning. In this case, the first words start the bullet in a hole. Unfortunately, completion of mandatory CBT requirements are, at best, membership level. Applying the two levels concept, if this is not a membership, most would score as fluff.

Author's Tip: *When using a lead-in, make it count. Consider the lead-in "base-wide mentor" or "base leader" if warranted. Both purport leadership. If supported by the ensuing words these are an effective start. Avoid the faulty lead-in trap.*

Example 3: The "led effort" trap

—**Led effort culminating in organization winning Air Force Verne Orr Award**

	Action	Impact	Result
Leadership	—	**winning Air Force Verne Orr Award**	
Management	—	—	—
Supervisory	—	—	—
Membership	—	—	—
Fluff	**Led effort culminating in organization**	—	

1/2 point–fluff; fluff–leadership. Winning the Air Force Verne Orr Award should be considered a leadership-level result. Unfortunately, in this example there is no way to know what the individual actually did, how they led, or the impact of their efforts. This example violates the TOS concept taught in chapter 4. Remember, action needs to be clearly explained to be effective.

Author's Tip: *The words "led effort" are ambiguous. Accomplishments need to be supported with concrete descriptions of the performance. This is a common writing flaw. Avoid the led effort trap.*

Example 4: The "job title" trap

—**Top 3 president; remarkable leadership that inspires esprit de corps**

	Action	Impact	Result
Leadership	**Top 3 president**	—	—
Management	—	—	—
Supervisory	—	—	—
Membership	—	—	—
Fluff	—	**remarkable leadership that inspires esprit de corps**	

0 points–leadership; fluff–fluff. This example shows exactly how not to document additional duties or other elected positions. Starting a bullet with a job title is used to qualify the action, impact, and results that may normally be outside normal duties. But the ensuing words must be provided so that appropriate value can be assigned.

> *Author's Tip*: *The words "Top 3 president," in this example, are a mini-job title. Without comments describing specific action and impact, how can we assess the performance? This would be like reading a performance appraisal with a job title but no statements to describe performance. Avoid the job title trap.*

Example 5: The "death bullet" trap

—Persistence impacted "outstanding" grade during compliance inspection

	Accomplishment	Impact
Leadership	—	"outstanding" grade during compliance inspection
Management	—	—
Supervisory	—	—
Membership	—	—
Fluff	**Persistence impacted**	—

1/2 point–fluff; leadership. This is similar to the led effort trap. The outstanding grade on the inspection denotes a leadership-level result, but the action and impact are vague. Thus, the assessment should be scored low or as fluff. The individual was there, but we do not know what he/she actually did. I call this the death bullet trap because it is prominent on performance reports and award nomination packages.

> *Author's Tip*: *Many appraisals cite stellar inspections and heralded actions. Sadly, writers are caught in the halo effect and forget to connect the dots. The TOS concept illustrates how this bullet skips from tactical to strategic level. Tie the action to the result. Avoid the death bullet trap.*

Example 6: The "lazy writing" trap

—LEAN-minded; process-mapped support section—tool issue more efficient

	Action	Impact	Result
Leadership	—	—	—
Management	—	process-mapped support section	—
Supervisory	—	—	—
Membership	—	—	tool issue more efficient
Fluff	LEAN-minded	—	—

<u>1/2 point–fluff; management–membership</u>. LEAN is a process improvement concept that focuses on eliminating unnecessary steps in a project. The result "more efficient" reflects lazy writing. Rather, convey how the process reduced time, minimized events per shift, or possibly yielded broader results.

> ***Author's Tip***: *Vague endings actually diminish other components in the bullet that add value. Endings such as* more efficient, sped process, reduced costs, *and* improved communication *are meaningless and provide no value. If you can just pull a result from thin air without research it likely falls in this category. Do your homework. Avoid the lazy writing trap.*

Example 7: The "too many acronyms" trap

—C5B SME; t/s elusive slat W/U; R2d #7B act <2 hrs—O/T real world msn

	Action	Impact	Result
Leadership	—	—	—
Management	—	—	—
Supervisory	—	—	—
Membership	—	—	—
Fluff	C5B SME; t/s elusive slat W/U; R2d #7B act <2 hrs—O/T real world msn		

0.0 point–fluff; fluff–fluff. This bullet says, C5B (aircraft) subject matter expert; troubleshoot elusive slat write up; remove and replaced #7B actuator in less than two hours. This allowed an on-time, real-word mission. One surefire way to limit the potential of an accomplishment is using too many acronyms.

> **Author's Tip**: *A good rule of thumb is to limit one or two acronyms per line. When acronyms become a distraction, or when the reader is forced to refer to an acronym list or research abbreviations on the Internet, these do not lead to positive outcomes. Avoid the too many acronyms trap.*

Example 8: The "bridge-too-far" trap

—Replaced rivets on cargo door; $2B fleet serviceable—C5s delivered supplies

	Action	Impact	Result
Leadership	—		$2B fleet serviceable—C5s delivered supplies
Management	—	—	—
Supervisory	—	—	—
Membership	Replaced rivets on cargo door		—
Fluff	—	—	—

1/2 point–membership; leadership–leadership. This example was described in chapter 4, which explained the TOS concept. The action does not connect well to the strategic-level results. Stretching action from one event to an entire fleet of aircraft is a bridge too far.

> **Author's Tip**: *Some writers embellish results. When this occurs, the embellished bullet—and possibly the entire package—may become suspect. Avoid the bridge-too-far trap.*

TOP 10 WRITING TRAPS | 65

Example 9: The "know your audience" trap

—Awarded LVN license! Passed requisite training and examinations within allotted time

	Result	Action	Impact
Leadership	—	—	—
Management	—	—	—
Supervisory	Awarded LVN License!		—
Membership	— Passed requisite training and examinations within allotted...
Fluff	—	—	—

1 point–supervisory; membership–membership. *Know your audience* means do not omit critical information. Most readers are unaware that licensed vocational nurse (LVN) certification is a two-year program that includes completion of oral, written and practical board examinations. Those in the medical field may know the requirements, but you should include pertinent details for an external audience. Sharing these additional facts will increase the value to board members. We described the need to include completion of "oral, written and practical board Examinations" which are more than one fact. The point here is, if you do not know your audience, spell out the details so everyone understands the scope of what they are reading.

> *Author's Tip*: *The trap here is the omission of critical information. Adding evidence to define the scope is beneficial to the reader when it increases value. Avoid the know-your-audience trap.*

Example 10: The "who's your audience" trap

—Completed final requirements for Org Behav bach deg with 3.87 GPA

	Action	Impact	Result
Leadership	—	—	—
Management	—	for Org Behav bach deg	—
Supervisory	—	—	with 3.87 GPA
Membership	Completed final requirements		
Fluff	—	—	—

1/2 point–membership; management–supervisory. Board members typically spend less than two minutes on selection folders. Similarly, human resource recruiters spend less than 15 seconds scouring resumes. In this example, the bell curve illustrates the most valuable component of the bullet. As you can see, the most important words (at the height of the bell curve) have been diminished to lowercase abbreviated words "bach deg." The bullet almost reads as though the individual completed a class versus a degree. How about starting the bullet "Awarded Bachelors!" You had me at hello.

> ***Author's Tip***: *You do not want to force time-constrained readers to hunt through your records to unearth your competencies and capabilities. Reorganize your accomplishments so the reviewer can fully and easily assess your performance and potential. Avoid the who's-your-audience trap.*

After reading this chapter you have the ability to recognize and avoid the 10 writing traps. As read by other board members, packages written by you will be recognized as straightforward, trustworthy, and professional.

Chapter 9

Perfect Practice Makes Perfect

Hard work often leads to success. No work seldom does.
—Harvey Mackay, businessman and writer

- *Remember to separate the facts from fiction and understand how to value portions of the bullet when elements are ambiguous. It gets trickier when the components in a bullet have varying performance levels.*
- *The categories in an award's package are not simply things to do; they should reflect the competencies commensurate with your grade, or higher. The same goes for performance reports, résumés, and any competency-based system.*
- *Challenge: Participate as an awards board member and learn to apply the fundamentals of scoring!*

This chapter is designed for purposeful practice. With the *magic* at hand, it's time to organize bullets into categories with insights and experience.

Experienced evaluators often see a common stumbling block among writers. This impediment deals with capturing the "what" in proper context. In this chapter, a series of practical exercises helps us avoid these contextual blunders.

Categories in awards packages and performance reports should reflect the competencies commensurate with your grade, or higher. The accomplishments that describe leading and developing people as well as managing systems and resources are captured in the top packages.

Three basic categories of accomplishments are found in most recognition packages: leadership and job performance in primary duty, significant self-improvement, and base and community involvement. While the specific details may change over time, a strong package will have mentoring bullets threaded throughout. Mentoring (internal and external) can be exemplified in any category. Now let's look at the categories with Chief Martin's observations.

Leadership and Job Performance in Primary Duty

This important category describes contributions toward the primary mission. That is why award packages require more examples in this category. These accomplishments describe how well the members performed their assigned primary and additional duties. This category includes illustrating the scope and level of responsibilities and the contribution to the mission and unit. Be sure to cite new initiatives or techniques developed by the member that positively affected the mission. Include contributions that resulted in Air Force-, major command-, and numbered Air Force-level inspections and/or evaluations.

> Just as the title alludes, evaluators are looking for leadership in the primary duty. If the bullets are centered on performance and not on leadership, then the maximum effect is not achieved. Obviously people can't lead everything they do; but it stands to reason, if their performance is being recognized, they must have demonstrated higher levels of performance during the award period. Also as the title alludes, the focus is on primary duty. The reader is comparing the nominee's grade, skill level, and duty title against their primary duty. Bullets that are not clearly part of their primary duty risk losing maximum effect. The fact this award package was submitted says the candidate is number one without saying it. I seriously doubt you are submitting your #5 technician instead of other higher performing individuals because it is their turn. Another point is to write what some call "job-related slang." As discussed previously, know your audience and write to it. It's hard for the reader to assign value to a bullet when the jargon isn't understood.
>
> —CMSgt James Martin, USAF, retired

Significant Self-improvement

Significant self-improvement describes training and on- and off-duty education. Describe how the member developed or improved skills related to primary duties including formal training, career development courses, on-the-job training, certifications, education related to primary duties, and so forth. Include completion of any professional military education as well as awards earned during in-residence attendance. Also include off-duty education such as completion of college classes, degree programs, and/or grade point average. Cite any other relevant training or activity that significantly enhanced the member's value as a military citizen. Consider how the member applied the education or training. Take account of force multiplication or how others were mentored and force development received a benefit.

> The key in this section is the words "significant" and "self." You see, it's easy to get wrapped up in developmental opportunities, but how it leads to your improvement is the key. Focus should also be on significant improvement so avoid physical fitness training and other training, which are part of your normal duties or contingency and readiness preparation, which are not considered significant, but required.
> —CMSgt James Martin, USAF, retired

Author's Tip: *The categories in an awards package are not simply things to do; they guide the competencies you are being evaluated against. The same goes for performance reports, résumés, and any competency-based system.*

Another key technique is to connect the education or training to the mission. For example, maybe someone attended a LEAN process improvement course and later applied the concepts to streamline one of the processes in the organization. Conversely, other times it may be better to clearly articulate completion of a course rather than trying to connect the impact of the 301-level psychology class to the mission.

Base and Community Involvement

Base and community involvement describes contributions toward the installation, Air Force, or the local community. Document improvements/involvement in base ceremonies, tradition, and heritage events when documenting base involvement. For community involvement, record contributions to local organizations—such as animal shelters or food banks—and impact to local towns or cities. This area defines the scope and impact of professional leadership and involvement in both the military and civilian community. Also include participation in unit advisory councils, professional military organizations, associations, and events. Examples include roles such as president of the Top 3 association, enlisted dining in/out committee, Air Force Sergeants Association activities, Sunday school teacher, parent-teacher association, and helping with any scout-related organizations.

When describing this section, I call it the "G.I. experience," with the G.I. standing for get involved! Believe it or not, depending on the nominees' rank and position, there are certain expectations to ensure our heritage and traditions are not forgotten.

—CMSgt James Martin, USAF, retired

Mentoring

This describes contributions involving internal and external mentoring. Internal mentoring develops Airmen within the member's organization. Describe how the member has shaped careers, built roadmaps for success, and led unit members toward training, promotion, education, and professional development. For external mentoring, describe contributions involving Airmen across the base. Include participation in seminars, panels, speaking engagements, and other opportunities that inspired or led or developed junior members, enlisted, civilians, officers, and cadets outside the member's organization. While a category for mentoring is not typically found on award packages, the significance of the involvement is paramount to sharing the many lessons learned during your career and developing future leaders.

Practice Bullets

The following pages contain a variety of examples describing accomplishments in every category and at every level of performance. Your task is to use the line-by-line scoring techniques to evaluate the bullet and assign performance levels to each component. By practicing, the categories and competencies are made clear.

Example 1 is already scored. Following example 1, use a pencil to write the corresponding performance levels in each example. Then compare your assessment to the answers recorded in the book. Remember the two-levels concept. Are we close?

Leadership and Job Performance in Primary Duty
Example 1: 1/2 point—Membership

—Built continuity book; captured lessons learned—processes more efficient

	Action	Impact	Result
Leadership	—	—	—
Management	—	—	—
Supervisory	—	—	—
Membership	Built continuity book; captured lessons learned		
Fluff	—	—	processes more efficient

You cannot give credit when actions are not observed. Vague and ambiguous language should not be rewarded. Spend the time to cite the facts appropriately and then support the results. As demonstrated in example 1, the lack of clarity for "process more efficient" resulted in fluff and zero value.

> *Author's Tip*: Look out for statements written to imply higher levels of performance, but in which the accomplishments are not supported with corresponding action, impact, or result.

Example 2

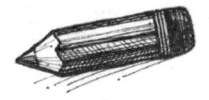

Use a pencil to write bullet components adjacent to the corresponding performance level. Then compare your assessment.

—LEANd tool room; applied 5 S's to tool issue—new process cut 15 mins/person

	Action	Impact	Result
Leadership	—	—	—
Management	—	—	—
Supervisory	—	—	—
Membership	—	—	—
Fluff	—	—	—

Author's Tip: *This 3-part bullet is well supported. Consider the scope, duration, impact, and time invested in accomplishing the activity.*

Example 2: 1 1/2 points–Management

—LEANd tool room; applied 5 S's to tool issue—new process cut 15 mins/person

	Action	Impact	Result
Leadership	—	—	—
Management	LEANd tool room	—	new process cut 15 mins/person
Supervisory	—	applied 5 S's to tool issue	—
Membership	—	—	—
Fluff	—	—	—

This is an interesting bullet. A few more words for clarification would strengthen the process mapping activity. Using the two levels concept, management or supervisory level is appropriate since the process impacted multiple people. Imagine if the process was benchmarked Air Force-wide; it could be a leadership-level result.

> If you want to further strengthen the bullet, you could clarify how many people were affected by the action. Was it 20 people or 200? Saving 15 hours each for 200 people makes for a strong bullet.
> —CMSgt James Martin, USAF, retired

Author's Tip: *Even when the individual's action and involvement are not at the leadership level, contributions that clearly tie to leadership-level results become exponentially valuable.*

Example 3

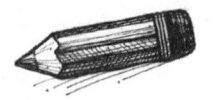

Use a pencil to write bullet components adjacent to the corresponding performance level. Then compare your assessment.

—Hard charging attitude culminated in unit winning USAF Verne Orr Award

	Accomplishment	Impact
Leadership	—	—
Management	—	—
Supervisory	—	—
Membership	—	—
Fluff	—	—

Author's Tip: Look out for statements written to imply higher levels of leadership, but accomplishments not are supported with corresponding action and impact.

Example 3: 1/2 point—membership (or fluff)

—Hard charging attitude culminated in unit winning USAF Verne Orr Award

	Accomplishment	Impact
Leadership	—	winning USAF Verne Orr Award
Management	—	—
Supervisory	—	—
Membership	—	—
Fluff	Hard charging attitude culminated in unit	

Even a membership-level score is gratuitous. Poorly written statements like these are death bullets documented in many performance appraisals and awards. Writers fall into the "halo effect" trap because they mention a significant award in the statement. Unit awards must be supported by the individual's contributions or no credit should be given. This is another example of the TOS concept. Just because a unit gets an award does not mean that the individual contributed toward the achievement. Basically the individual was there and may deserve membership level value just for being there.

> If the person contributed to the USAF Verne Orr Award the writer should describe how so. Tangible action that clearly connects to a powerful result is undeniable. Simply being a part of a unit that wins the award doesn't automatically afford everyone the accolades.
>
> —CMSgt James Martin, USAF, retired

Example 4

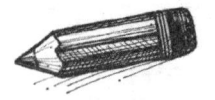

Use a pencil to write bullet components adjacent to the corresponding performance level. Then compare your assessment.

—AEF project officer; planned logistics/schedule—300 pers/20 tons cargo to AOR

	Accomplishment	Impact
Leadership	—	—
Management	—	—
Supervisory	—	—
Membership	—	—
Fluff	—	—

Though AEF is a common term, be sure the use of acronyms does not detract from the overall package. If the reader must research or go back and forth to a definition list, the merit of the accomplishment may be lost in translation.

> A way to rewrite this so the second accomplishment becomes an "impact" statement is to write 300 pers/20 tons of cargo prepped for deployment.
>
> —MSgt Casey T. Schoettmer, USAF, retired

Example 4: 1 1/2 points–Management

—AEF project officer; planned logistics/schedule—300 pers/20 tons cargo to AOR

	Accomplishment	*Impact*
Leadership	—	300 pers/20 tons cargo to AOR
Management	AEF project officer planned logistics/schedule	
Supervisory	—	—
Membership	—	—
Fluff	—	—

Author's Tip: This is a two-part bullet without a result. Regardless, the high-level responsibility and impact reflect significant competencies. The results may not materialize until after the deployment. This would be difficult to rate this lower than management using the two levels concept.

Significant Self-Improvement

Example 5

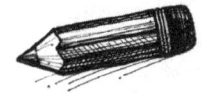

Use a pencil to write bullet components adjacent to the corresponding performance level. Then compare your assessment.

—Completed College Math CLEP; received six credits toward associate's degree

	Accomplishment	Impact
Leadership	—	—
Management	—	—
Supervisory	—	—
Membership	—	—
Fluff	—	—

Author's Tip: *A College Level Examination Program (CLEP) is a building block in the education process.*

Example 5: 1/2 point–Membership

— **Completed College Math CLEP; received six credits toward associate's degree**

	Accomplishment	*Impact*
Leadership	—	—
Management	—	—
Supervisory	—	—
Membership	Completed College Math CLEP; received six credits toward…	
Fluff	—	—

This example has two components—impact and accomplishment. Completion of a CLEP exam is six credits toward a degree—a building block toward a larger educational milestone.

> To possibly strengthen this bullet, one could state how many classes away from the milestone the member is. This shows effort and enduring dedication. Some readers don't agree with listing it as a CLEP as it doesn't carry the same message as attending a class for weeks. However, since an accredited college accepts CLEP as an equivalency to their in-residence requirement, then so should we. A better technique may be to state, "completed college math" and leave it at that.
>
> —CMSgt James Martin, USAF, retired

Author's Tip: *Completing a CLEP exam puts the member on the way toward achieving a degree. But one CLEP is a small building block of a larger accomplishment so it reflects membership-level performance.*

Example 6

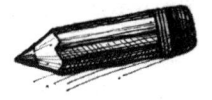

Use a pencil to write bullet components adjacent to the corresponding performance level. Then compare your assessment.

—Awarded CCAF degree! Completed two classes to satisfy final requirements

	Result	Action	Impact
Leadership	—	—	—
Management	—	—	—
Supervisory	—	—	—
Membership	—	—	—
Fluff	—	—	—

Author's Tip: *This is a three-part bullet with components arranged in reverse format.*

Example 6: 1 point–Supervisory

—Awarded CCAF degree! Completed two classes to satisfy final requirements

	Result	Action	Impact
Leadership	—	—	—
Management	Awarded CCAF degree!	—	—
Supervisory	—	—	—
Membership	—	completed two classes to satisfy final requirements	
Fluff	—	—	—

Supervisory level best describes this accomplishment. Scoring is not a perfect science. However, the most important component of this bullet is the award of a Community College of the Air Force (CCAF) degree and the individual's contributions directly tie into that result.

Author's Tip: Another consideration is the rank of the individual. Completion of a CCAF degree might not carry as much weight for a senior NCO as it would for a junior Airman.

Example 7

Use a pencil to write bullet components alongside the corresponding performance level. Then compare your assessment.

—**Finished 2-year program; awarded FAA Airframe and Powerplant (A&P) license**

	Accomplishment	Impact
Leadership	—	—
Management	—	—
Supervisory	—	—
Membership	—	—
Fluff	—	—

Author's Tip: Look out for statements written to imply higher levels of leadership but lack supporting evidence showing accomplishment corresponds with impact.

Author's Tip: This is an important example of knowing your audience. Readers who are not in the aviation industry may not know the scope or duration to earn a Federal Aviation Administration (FAA) A&P license.

Example 7: 1 1/2 points–Management

—Finished 2-year program; awarded FAA Airframe and Powerplant (A&P) license

	Accomplishment	*Impact*
Leadership	—	—
Management	**Finished 2-year program**	—
Supervisory	—	**awarded FAA Airframe and Powerplant (A&P)...**
Membership	—	—
Fluff	—	—

This is a great self-improvement bullet for an aircraft maintenance technician. The program is valuable as it directly contributes to the mission and career field.

> An important self-improvement note is whether it contributes to the career field. There are instances where people are pursuing goals that do not necessarily contribute to their immediate duty but toward long-term personal goals. Either way, ensure the intent is captured so the reader is not confused. Developing this further, one can show how this accomplishment contributed to both personal and professional development.
>
> —CMSgt James Martin, USAF, retired

Author's Tip: The bullet describes the license as a two-year program. That should provide some measure to help assess the value the accomplishment. Using the two levels concept, were we close?

Example 8

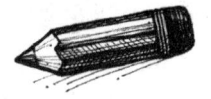

Use a pencil to write bullet components adjacent to the corresponding performance level. Then compare your assessment.

— **John Levitow winner! Awarded "Top Graduate" during 6-week SNCO Academy**

	Result	*Action*	*Impact*
Leadership	—	—	—
Management	—	—	—
Supervisory	—	—	—
Membership	—	—	—
Fluff	—	—	—

Author's Tip: *This 3-part bullet is rearranged following the who's-your-audience trap to highlight the strengths at the beginning of the bullet.*

Example 8: 2 points–Leadership

—John Levitow winner! Awarded "Top Graduate" during 6-week SNCO Academy

	Result	Action	Impact
Leadership	John Levitow winner!	Awarded "Top Graduate"	
Management	—	—	—
Supervisory	—	—	**during 6-week SNCO Academy**
Membership	—	—	—
Fluff	—	—	—

Do not allow the supervisory-level impact to affect the value of this bullet. Scoring is not a checklist process; it is a guide to help identify the strengths and weaknesses in the bullet. Clearly, the John Levitow winner at the SNCO Academy warrants a leadership-level score. To further strengthen this accomplishment, one can discuss the class size competing for this honor.

> ***Author's Tip****: Do not conceal a top graduate award or other significant results in the middle or end of the bullet. Instead, align the best part of the bullet at the beginning so that it's not missed.*

Base and Community Involvement

Example 9

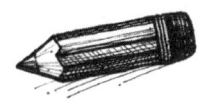

Use a pencil to write bullet components adjacent to the corresponding performance level. Then compare your assessment.

—SecAF visit lead; chaired wing committee—planned 5 major events/12 unit tours

	Action	Impact	Result
Leadership	—	—	—
Management	—	—	—
Supervisory	—	—	—
Membership	—	—	—
Fluff	—	—	—

Author's Tip: This is a 3-part bullet. The action "Secretary of the Air Force visit lead" is actually a mini-job title. A mini job title is used to qualify the action, impact, and results that may normally be outside normal duties.

Example 9: 2 points–Leadership

—SecAF visit lead; chaired wing committee—planned 5 major events/12 unit tours

	Action	Impact	Result
Leadership	SecAF visit lead;	planned 5 major events/12 unit tours	
Management	—	chaired wing committee	
Supervisory	—	—	—
Membership	—	—	—
Fluff	—	—	—

This is a top-level accomplishment. The person leading the Secretary of the Air Force visit is hand-selected.

> If you want to further strengthen the bullet, you could add the impact or the outcome of the visit and the how the individual contributed to the outcome.
>
> —CMSgt James Martin, USAF, retired

Author's Tip*: This is a strong accomplishment that demonstrates a high level of responsibility. This performance clearly exemplifies general competencies expected of a senior NCO ready for promotion to the next higher grade.*

Example 10

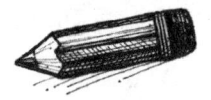

Use a pencil to write bullet components adjacent to the corresponding performance level. Then compare your assessment.

—Led carwash fundraiser; organized people/logistics—raised $200 for party

	Action	Impact	Result
Leadership	—	—	—
Management	—	—	—
Supervisory	—	—	—
Membership	—	—	—
Fluff	—	—	—

Author's Tip: *This bullet is well supported. Although the word led was used, the reader needs to consider the scope of the project to determine the appropriate context to assign a performance level.*

Example 10: 1 point–supervisory

—Led carwash fundraiser; organized people/logistics—raised $200 for party

	Action	Impact	Result
Leadership	—	—	—
Management	—	—	—
Supervisory	Led carwash fundraiser; organized people/logistics		
Membership	—	—	raised $200 for party
Fluff	—	—	—

Supervisory-level action and impact best describes this accomplishment. The words describing impact may be perceived as management level, but the $200 result is membership level, resulting in an overall supervisory performance level.

Author's Tip: To clarify ambiguous components always think in terms of two levels. Consider the impact in this bullet: if organized people/logistics for a car wash was not management level, then what? Leadership level would be a stretch, and the scope of the effort leads back to supervisory level (small team / small program). The two levels concept helps to frame the overall context of the accomplishment.

Example 11

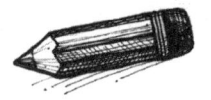

Use a pencil to write bullet components adjacent to the corresponding performance level. Compare your assessment.

—Chaired banquet committee; led 25 people—planned event for 300 guests

	Action	Impact	Result
Leadership	—	—	—
Management	—	—	—
Supervisory	—	—	—
Membership	—	—	—
Fluff	—	—	—

Author's Tip: This bullet is well supported with the number of people "guided" and the impact of the event.

Example 11: 1 1/2 points–Management

—Chaired banquet committee; led 25 people—planned event for 300 guests

	Action	Impact	Result
Leadership	—	—	—
Management	Chaired banquet committee; led 25 people		
Supervisory	—	—	planned event for 300 guests
Membership	—	—	—
Fluff	—	—	—

Did the two level concept help on this example? The overall bullet is sound at the management level. There is enough information to see the level of performance. However, the value could go up or down based on the rank of the individual leading the committee. It would be very hard to imagine someone scoring membership level.

Author's Tip: This bullet can be strengthened with more impact and result information supporting a professional seminar, heritage, or history event. Also, consider if VIPs were engaged like the mayor, flag officers, or dignitaries.

Example 12

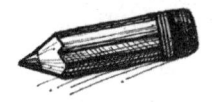

Use a pencil to write bullet components adjacent to the corresponding performance level. Compare your assessment.

—Top 3 pres; unified 165 members; managed progress/executed 65 events

	Action	Impact	Result
Leadership	—	—	—
Management	—	—	—
Supervisory	—	—	—
Membership	—	—	—
Fluff	—	—	—

> ***Author's Tip***: The words "Top 3 President" are a mini-job title. The title infers a certain level of leadership, but it must be supported with corresponding accomplishments.

Example 12: 2 points–Leadership

—Top 3 pres; unified 165 members; managed progress/executed 65 events

	Action	Impact	Result
Leadership	Top 3 pres		managed progress/executed 65 base events
Management	—	unified 165 members	—
Supervisory	—	—	—
Membership	—	—	—
Fluff	—	—	—

Author's Tip: *No ambiguity here. The words Top 3 president are supported with strong action, impact, and results.*

Mentoring

Example 13

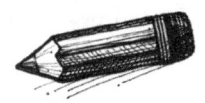

Use a pencil to write bullet components adjacent to the corresponding performance level. Compare your assessment.

—Mentored 3 Airmen; taught writing tips—eliminated rewrites by 20%

	Action	Impact	Result
Leadership	—	—	—
Management	—	—	—
Supervisory	—	—	—
Membership	—	—	—
Fluff	—	—	—

Author's Tip: Consider the rank of the individual teaching the Airmen and whether or not the term Airmen contextually refers to E-4 and below or if it is used generically for all ranks.

Example 13: 1/2 point–Membership

—Mentored 3 Airmen; taught writing tips—eliminated rewrites by 20%

	Action	Impact	Result
Leadership	—	—	—
Management	—	—	—
Supervisory	**Mentored 3 Airmen**	—	**eliminated rewrites by 20%**
Membership	—	**taught writing tips**	—
Fluff	—	—	—

In this example, the action and result are considered supervisory level since teaching your subordinates is a basic expectation of a supervisor.

> To further strengthen this bullet, the impact may shift from decreasing rewrites by 20% to explain how the action restored an established standard of excellence. If the writing issue was severely dysfunctional, then merely improving by 20% may not have improved enough. Be sure to describe the relevance of the 20%. Another example is if we decrease safety incidents by 20%, one could conclude we still have safety incidences as we didn't eliminate them completely. In this case, are the remaining safety incidents acceptable?
>
> —CMSgt James Martin, USAF, retired

Example 14

Use a pencil to write bullet components adjacent to the corresponding performance level. Compare your assessment.

—Facilitated seminar; taught writing course—molded 36 future supervisors

	Action	Impact	Result
Leadership	—	—	—
Management	—	—	—
Supervisory	—	—	—
Membership	—	—	—
Fluff	—	—	—

Author's Tip*: Consider the scope, duration, and time invested in accomplishing the activity.*

Example 14: 1 point–Supervisory

— Facilitated seminar; taught writing course—molded 36 future supervisors

	Action	Impact	Result
Leadership	—	—	—
Management	—	—	—
Supervisory	Facilitated seminar; taught writing course	— molded 36 future...	
Membership	—	—	—
Fluff	—	—	—

Supervisory-level action, impact, and result best describe this accomplishment. This is a one-time event taking one hour to accomplish. The amount of time preparing for the class is unknown. Potentially, the writer could have described how the individual created a lesson plan. That added information might increase the value of the action to management level if additional competencies are demonstrated.

> ***Author's Tip***: *This bullet describes application of competencies expected of NCOs and senior NCOs. Variables added can steer this into any one of the three primary categories. As written, it flows into primary duty. As the member's first presentation after receiving facilitation training, it can be self-improvement. Finally, if the context is off-base JROTC development, it's community involvement.*

Example 15

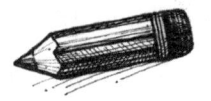

Use a pencil to write bullet components adjacent to the corresponding performance level. Compare your assessment.

—Led 5-day orientation course; planned development seminar for 100 people

	Accomplishment	Impact
Leadership	—	—
Management	—	—
Supervisory	—	—
Membership	—	—
Fluff	—	—

Author's Tip: This is a strong accomplishment demonstrating management-level competencies.

Example 15: 1 1/2 points–Management

—Led 5-day orientation course; planned development seminar for 100 people

	Accomplishment	Impact
Leadership	—	—
Management	**Led 5-day orientation course; planned development seminar for 100 people**	
Supervisory	—	—
Membership	—	—
Fluff	—	—

This example resulted in a management-level score. The accomplishment is management level, and using the two level concept, the impact would be supervisory/management level.

> To further strengthen this bullet, the writer can clarify the impact of the weeklong course to provide more leadership involvement. How many competencies taught to the students? Who are the students?
>
> —CMSgt James Martin, USAF, retired

Example 16

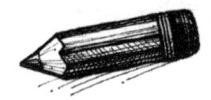

Use a pencil to write bullet components adjacent to the corresponding performance level. Compare your assessment.

—Base mentor; taught NCOPE, ROTC, ALS, FTAC—shaped 325 future leaders

	Action	Impact	Result
Leadership	—	—	—
Management	—	—	—
Supervisory	—	—	—
Membership	—	—	—
Fluff	—	—	—

Author's Tip: *The use of acronyms should be kept to a minimum. Be sure they do not detract from the overall package. If the reader has to study or constantly review a definition list, the merit of the accomplishment becomes lost in translation.*

Example 16: 2 points–Leadership

—Base mentor; taught NCOPE, ROTC, ALS, FTAC—shaped 325 future leaders

	Action	Impact	Result
Leadership	Base mentor	—	shaped 325 future leaders
Management	—	taught NCOPE, ROTC, ALS, FTAC	—
Supervisory	—	—	—
Membership	—	—	—
Fluff	—	—	—

To strengthen this, the writer can include the frequency if applicable. If 325 were taught during four or six seminars, the inferred diligence and dedication sends an even stronger message. Then it's not looked at as a one-time event.

—CMSgt James Martin, USAF, retired

Author's Tip: In this example, the lead in base mentor is supported by the action and result placing the competency at the leadership level. The person is involved in professional enhancement (PE) seminars, Airmen leadership schools (ALS), First-Term Airmen Center (FTAC), and the reserve officer training corps (ROTC). This exemplifies a high level of mentoring and involvement.

Summary

When writing bullets, remember the competencies are expected to match the rank and grade of the individual. These competencies set the stage for the performance levels and categories of which you should write. Remove ambiguity and minimize general statements to create a more significant package. Emphasize the action by tying the performance to the impact or result. Now with well-written bullets packaged neatly into proper categories, it is time to consider the board process. The last chapter reviews a basic board process, which includes how to resolve disputes and tiebreakers.

Note

1. K. Anders Ericsson, Ralph T. Krampe, and Clemens Tesch-Romer, "The Role of Deliberate Practice in the Acquisition of Expert Performance," *Psychological Review* 100, no. 3 (January 1993): 363–406.

Part 4

Conducting Boards

When leaders yield, there is no resistance, when leaders insist there is no yielding.
—Ulysses S. Grant

Part 4 includes a bonus chapter that teaches a fair and consistent approach to conducting boards. This part focuses on a contentious topic, the tie-breaking process.

As in any business endeavor, board members need to get beyond positional obligations to discuss the underlying interests. If professionals cannot get past their ego, then the best outcome is diminished and the process may come to a halt. If a picture is worth a thousand words, allow me to paint a story.

Chapter 10

You Just Can't Make This Up

In 2002 four of us were involved in an annual awards board that ended in a tie. I was perplexed because the scores were not close, based on my scoring—the ones taught in this book. Back then, annual awards took up both sides of a nomination package and comprised almost 80 lines of information.

Package A weighed in at nearly 95 points. Package B, purportedly tied, amassed only 35 points using the same scoring system taught in this book. Yes, 35 points meant package B was bad, really bad. Most of the lines, one after another, were fluff. And those lines that were not fluff were not good.

As the board discussed the merits of the tied packages, I noticed two of the board members were relating their thoughts from clean sheets of paper. No notes, no marks—just a score on the top of the page that boiled 80 lines of information down to one numerical value. It had been two weeks since the scores were turned in; so, these members must have good memories.

Looking back to my packages, every line was underlined and circled, and scores were placed in the margin suggesting strengths and weaknesses.

One board member said he "really" liked package B and cited one of the accomplishments.

Glancing to the margin on my corresponding package, I recognized the merit of that line and assigned a zero. I also noticed that 25 other lines in package B were fluff. The board member read the statement that had impressed him, "Volunteered to attend professional military education school early." I pointed out how this and so many other bullets were unsupported and lacking in any factual information—any tangible action. Further investigation revealed he did not actually go to school. He only volunteered.

Conversely, package A was loaded with management- and leadership-level contributions. It was easy to find the 1-1/2s and 2s in the margin and then match the underlined words that identified the strengths. This is probably a good time to point out the package-A nominee was not from my organization.

I scratched my head and pointed out that package A only had two lines of fluff compared to 25 lines in package B. The other board member replied, "Yeah, but I really, really like package B." Oh, consecutive "reallys!"

Imagine package B littered in circles, a method to highlight weak or unsupported accomplishments. I realized the board member did not have a good memory, and he just did not know what he was doing.

In any dispute process, positions must be supported by merit. Discussions cannot be based on how much you *really, really like* a certain package (or person).

Bottom line: package B was filled with fluff, and the other board member did not want to discuss—or was unable to discuss—underlying interests. Without telling you how the board ended, just know I had a few sleepless nights.

I thought the tiebreaker was going to be easy; unfortunately, our awards program did not have provisions for such disputes. We went back and forth advocating packages and never made headway.

What does it all mean? I stand by the benefits of a consistent approach, as it leads to a fair outcome—certainly a fairer process than the personal preference method.

> **Author's Tip**: *The best way to resolve disputes is to prevent them. Use line-by-line scoring with clear guidance and a consistent process.*

Ben Franklin prolifically stated, "An ounce of prevention is worth a pound of cure." Most organizations have basic guidance for boards. Experience shows it is a gram of prevention instead of an ounce. Guidance typically does not include preboard training or setup. Even if it does, many board members are not adequately trained in the consistent process as described in this book.

> I have taught Chief Jaren's system to more than 600 Airmen, NCOs, and Senior NCOs over the last three years. In doing so several second- and third-order effects have come from this instruction. One ancillary lesson is the enduring principle that when grading packages facts will beat emotion every time. How students feel about a bullet fails in the presence of other students using this system. Furthermore, by only providing limited facts, the same way performance reports and recognition packages are often submitted, students become frustrated. Their annoyance drives home the principle that what is on the 1206 is what is graded, nothing more, and nothing less.
>
> —MSgt Justin Deisch, USAF

The key principles in this book will provide the ounce of prevention. Referring back to the previous chapters, the highlights of any board process should include:

1. Line-by-line scoring. Each accomplishment should be scored on its own merit. This also helps in the tie-breaking process.
2. Performance levels. The numbering system isn't important. Consistent line-by-line scoring by all board members is needed to minimize bias.
3. Board training and setup. Whatever measures are used, ensure board members are aligned. Consider a few sample bullets to standardize the team before beginning the review.

So what about tie-breakers? Because packages are tightly competitive, ties are inevitably going to occur. Fortunately, through our experiences, the group awards' instruction was rewritten to include the tenets of the 715th Air Mobility Squadron awards scoring system. We also added the dispute resolution process.

Bonus Chapter

The author provides an online bonus chapter that encompasses a basic board process, including how to resolve disputes and deal with tiebreakers. This chapter is available for download on http://www.BrownBagLessons.com.

Conclusion

Whether you are an accomplished writer or a novice, you will see the merit in the approach. This book does not teach how to write a bullet. It teaches how to write a powerful bullet. It unlocks a secret that has benefited thousands. Now, I trust that it will benefit you.

Throughout a long career, you tend to learn a trick or two. At times, a mentor or supervisor shares tricks of the trade. Regrettably, we often learn from the school of hard knocks. Fortunately, every once in a while, a bit of luck comes your way. *The magic* contained herein teaches a critical eye, and the result is the composition of a powerful bullet.

You now have a simple three-step process to identify the strengths and weaknesses in a bullet. You not only learned how to write but also, more importantly, you honed a critical eye and learned what *not* to write!

Thousands of people have benefited from this information. Armed with these tried-and-true principles, you will hold the key to putting the power in your pen. The key is to write bullets accurately while truly capturing the accomplishments of your people. That is what it is all about—documenting the hard work and accomplishments that our people do, day in and day out.

After a 30-year Air Force career, and as someone who has traveled just a bit further down the road, I humbly offer to you my *Brown Bag Lessons*.

Warm regards,

Eric Jaren

Abbreviations

A&P	Airframe and Powerplant
AEF	air and space expeditionary force
AI	accomplishment-impact
AIR	action-impact-result
ALS	Airman Leadership School
AOR	area of responsibility
BDOC C3	Base Defense Operations Center, command, control, and communications
CAS	close air support
CBT	computer-based training
CCAF	Community College of the Air Force
CFC	Combined Federal Campaign
CGO	company grade officer
CLEP	College-Level Examination Program
CSAF	chief of staff of the Air Force
EPR	enlisted performance report
FAA	Federal Aviation Administration
FTAC	First-Term Airman Center
GPA	grade point average
JROTC	Junior Reserve Officer Training Corps
LVN	licensed vocational nurse
NCO	noncommissioned officer
NCOPE	NCO professional enhancement
PE	professional enhancement
PERSCO	personnel support for contingency operations
R2d	removed and replaced
ROTC	Reserve Officer Training Corps

SecAF	Secretary of the Air Force
SME	subject matter expert
SNCOA	Senior Noncommissioned Officer Academy
SOS	Squadron Officer School
t/s	troubleshoot
TOS	tactical-operational-strategic
TTP	techniques, tactics, and procedures
UCI	unit compliance inspection
W/U	write up

Appendix

Further Resources

Readers should visit www.brownbaglessons.com to access additional information. This site provides free training aids, course materials, and other tools to facilitate *Brown Bag Lessons*.

Keep an eye out for more *Brown Bag Lessons*.

Contact Information

www.linkedin.com/in/ericjaren
www.brownbaglessons.com/